PRENTICE-HALL
FOUNDATIONS OF CATHOLIC THEOLOGY SERIES

THE IMAGE OF GOD IN CREATION, by Sister M. Charles Borromeo Muckenhirn, CSC

THE WORD MADE FLESH, by David J. Bowman, SJ

SACRAMENTS OF INITIATION, by Henry J. D'Aoust, OSB

THE ONE GOD, by Wilfrid F. Dewan, CSP

CHRIST'S REDEMPTIVE SACRIFICE, by William F. Hogan

SIGNS OF TRANSFORMATION IN CHRIST, by John H. Miller, CSC

THE ISRAEL OF GOD, by John M. Oesterreicher

SACRAMENTS OF HEALING AND OF VOCATION, by Paul F. Palmer, SJ

ESCHATOLOGY, by John J. Quinn

THE CHURCH OF CHRIST, by Maurice Bonaventure Schepers, OP

THE THREE PERSONS IN ONE GOD, by Gerard S. Sloyan

THE LIFE OF GRACE, by P. Gregory Stevens, OSB

FOUNDATIONS OF CATHOLIC THEOLOGY SERIES

Gerard S. Sloyan, *Editor*

CHRIST'S REDEMPTIVE SACRIFICE

WILLIAM F. HOGAN

Immaculate Conception Seminary
Darlington, N.J.

PRENTICE-HALL, INC.
Englewood Cliffs, N.J.

Nihil obstat:

Robert E. Hunt, STD
Censor Librorum

Imprimatur:

✠ Thomas A. Boland, STD
Archbishop of Newark

April 8, 1963

 Library of Congress Catalog Card No.: 63-17628.

PRENTICE-HALL INTERNATIONAL, INC., LONDON
PRENTICE-HALL OF AUSTRALIA, PTY., LTD., SYDNEY
PRENTICE-HALL OF CANADA, LTD., TORONTO
PRENTICE-HALL OF INDIA (PRIVATE) LTD., NEW DELHI
PRENTICE-HALL OF JAPAN, INC., TOKYO
PRENTICE-HALL DE MEXICO, S.A., MEXICO CITY

Third printing......August, 1964

Photo: Apse of Benedictine Monastery, Monreale, Sicily (twelfth century). Courtesy Raymond V. Schoder, SJ

C 13361

EDITOR'S NOTE

This series offers the depth and richness of the divine message of salvation proclaimed to us by Christ. The theology, or "faith seeking understanding," contained here is not on a catechetical level, nor yet on a complex, higher level; it is clear and nontechnical, but at the same time adult and thorough. It is a scholarly presentation of revelation.

These volumes do not adopt an apologetic approach. They

neither attempt to justify Catholic faith nor aim at convincing those who do not profess it of the reasonableness of believing. This series is written primarily for those who already believe, who accept the Church as the living continuation of Christ, and the Scriptures as divinely inspired.

The authors do not attempt a philosophy of God or of Christianity, but a study of the mystery of God seen through the eyes of faith. The mystery of faith will not be dispelled by the study of these books. It will remain.

Since some background in philosophy on the part of the reader is needed, and cannot in every case be presumed, there are times when philosophical terms will need to be explained. Philosophical reasoning is very much a part of speculative theology.

Although the breakdown of the series is along traditional lines, each volume is designed to emphasize the oneness of God's plan of salvation and not its different facets. Distinction is made in order to unite. What is taught in the Scriptures is stressed, so that it may be seen how men of the Bible understood the message entrusted to them. The historical aspects of doctrine as held by Christians are then treated: the testimony of the early Christian writers and the liturgy to the belief of the Church; the controversies and heresies that necessitated defense and precise formulation, and finally, the magisterial teaching in each subject area. In this way speculative theology, or the present understanding of each mystery, is not seen in isolation from the sources of faith.

Thus, the revealed Christian message is viewed as the *tradition* (in the fullest and best sense of that theological term) expressed in and through the Church over the centuries—more explicitly formulated, from age to age, and with further applications. But it is still the same saving message begun in the Old Testament and perfected in the mystery and person of Jesus Christ.

One last point is important. Although the study of theology is an exercise of intellect, it can never be exclusively this. The message of Jesus Christ is a living Word, an invitation to participate in the saving event of the redemption, starting in this world by faith and the union of grace, and culminating in heaven by vision and immediate union. This invitation demands response or living faith. The study of the Christian message through theology requires such response, for the message is not something that was heard and assented to once. It is a Word addressed to us that requires our vigorous "Yes" for a lifetime.

CONTENTS

CHAPTER ONE

THE NEW ADAM

Any theological inquiry into the redemptive sacrifice of Christ begins with locating Christ in the history of man and in the plan of God. This sacrifice as it affects man may be described as the establishment of man in a state of sonship. Since, in the actual order of things, it also includes the rescue of man by God from sin, it is important to establish sin as a fact of man's history and determine the nature of sin's impact on him. This study should make it easier to assess the meaning and value of Christ's redemptive activity. The theological consideration of man in sin leads to the conclusion that he can be extracted from it only by God. The helplessness of man in sin, and the fact that God did take the initiative to rescue him, bring the incarnation and the saving work of Christ into perspective. This perspective must be established and maintained throughout our study of the redemption. Any blurring of the lines of these facts of sin and God's initiative will distort the believer's picture of the redemptive sacrifice of Christ.

St. Paul brings these facts into focus when he refers to Christ as the last (or second) Adam, calling the first one "a type of him who was to come." (Rom 5,9–21; 1 Cor 15) This insight into Christ's life and work points up his critical function in history—to correct the damage done to all men in Adam, their common father. The disobedience of the first man made all men sinners and introduced death into the world. The obedience of Christ offsets this tragedy and results in "the sanctification giving life to all men." (Rom 5,18) This theme is taken up by the Church in the blessing of the paschal candle when she sings the praises of "Our Lord Jesus Christ who paid for us to his eternal Father the debt of Adam, and by his merciful blood cancelled the guilt incurred by original sin." (Easter Song, *Exsultet*)

One of the major tasks of this volume will be to work out the implications of Christ's work as the Second Adam. This is best begun by studying the first Adam and measuring with some exactness the effect he has had on all men. Such a study specifies the investigation of sin as a fact of human history and determines the needs of man in sin. It also describes the situation from which Christ rescued the human race. The coming of the New Adam as a corrective for man's sinful condition brings into focus the fact that he represents a divine intervention in human history. The New Adam cannot be understood unless we realize that he has been provided by God, and that his entrance into the history of man is the climax of God's plan of rescue. The present chapter is concerned with two matters, first, Adam's effect on the human race, and second, the initiative of God to correct the situation of man in sin.

THE CHILDREN OF ADAM

The Fact of Sin

Under the pressures of Pelagianism and Protestantism the Church has examined the primitive condition of man. In the Councils of Carthage (418), Orange (529), and Trent (1546) she underlined two important facts of that history. The first is that the beginnings of man's history were marked by his friendship with God. In addition to his very considerable human powers, man was adorned by God with a new and higher principle of life which took him beyond the boundaries of human nature, made him more than a creature, and drew him into an intimate familiarity with God. It made him capable of achieving the destiny of the "face to face" vision of God. This life was accompanied by other gifts, called preternatural, which perfected man within the boundaries of his nature, giving him an immunity from death, ignorance, suffering and concupiscence. It was God's design that these gifts, both supernatural (that is, grace) and preternatural, be inherited by all the descendants of the first man. Every human being was destined to enter the world a friend of God in a way that exceeded all man's natural powers and needs. (D192, 788, 1021)

The second fact is that quite early in his history man interrupted this friendship by offending deliberately against the love of God his Father. The effects of this offense against filial love were calamitous. While retaining a basic orientation to his high destiny, man forfeited the life of grace needed to achieve that destiny. He estranged himself from God and lost the preternatural gifts. Mysteriously, this calamity touched all other men. The descendants of Adam begin their existence destined for the vision of God but inevitably estranged from him and incapable of this vision because of their inherited sin. (D788ff)

Another effect of this primitive disaster is the personal sins of all men. The Church teaches that even when the petition "forgive us our debts" is spoken by saints it is in place; there is no man without sin and no man who cannot truthfully ask for the forgiveness of his personal sins. (D107) The universal inclination to sin derives from the sin of the first man, said the Council of Trent (D792); therefore, personal sins are consequent upon the sin of Adam.

This developed doctrine of the Church has its roots in the Genesis narrative. (Cf. *The Image of God in Creation* in this series.) The detailed description of the first man's sin with its effects in his person and life (Gn 3) is followed closely by the accounts of the first murder (Gn 4) and the sin of the sons of God and the daughters of men. (Gn 6) The deep consciousness of a universal moral misery into which Adam's sin had thrust all men is seen in the reflections attributed to God before the deluge (Gn 6,5) and again before the covenant with Noa. (Gn 8,21)

The endurance of this consciousness and the recognition of the inevitability of man's sinful condition can be seen at a much later date. (Ps 50[51],7; 57[58],4) St. Paul's testimony to the universal effects of Adam's sin shows that he is heir to this consciousness of sin and that it is pivotal in his thinking. (Rom 5,12–21)

The Reign of Sin

St. Paul describes humanity in sin with genuine dramatic force. His thesis is, in brief: "All have sinned and have need of the glory of God." (Rom 3,23) This statement is the climax of a long and strongly worded indictment of all men. Speaking first of the pagans, he condemns their rejection of God and their addiction to idolatry. (Rom 1,18–23) Then he sketches the depravity of the pagan world and gives a devastating list of the sins of the pagans. (Rom 1,24–32) Turning to the Jews, apparently favored by God, he quickly exposes them: "For you who pass judgment do the same things yourself." (Rom 2,1) Their privileges have not saved the Jews from sin but only compounded their guilt, as their own history testifies. (Rom 3,11–18) There is no man without sin, "for we have argued that the Jews and the Greeks are all under the domination of sin. . . ." (Rom 3,10)

Going beyond the sinful acts of all men, Paul refers to sin as a power that is outside and above the individual man. Sin personified (*hē hamartía*) enters the world as a result of the transgression of the first man. Such is the power of this sin that it brings a threefold death to men: the death of their souls, death in their bodies, and the ultimate death of damnation. Thus does *hē hamartía* bring ruin to man, with the personal sins of all men, themselves a consequence of *hē harmartía,* contributing to the disaster. (Rom 5,12) Sin personified is a despot ruling in men and enslaving them (Rom 6,16; cf. Jn 8,34); it is a tyrant to whom men have been sold (Rom 7,14), a master taking possession of the human body to make its members his instruments. (Rom 7,17–23)

The figure of sin as a living, malignant spirit tyrannizing all men is effective in portraying humanity under the influence of Adam. It conveys a sense of the massiveness of sin, its vitality and the universal influence it has exerted on man. Apart from any personification of sin, Paul outlines the tragic effects of sin quite systematically: "Therefore as from the offense of the one man the result was condemnation to all men. . . . Just as by the disobedience of the one man the many were constituted sinners. . . ." (Rom 5,18f) This description of humanity after the fall was basic to the thinking of the Church when the councils carefully formulated the description of man's sinful condition. It was undoubtedly the inspiration of St. Augustine's chilling description of mankind: "the condemned mass of the human race . . . being thrown from evils to new evils." (*On Faith, Hope, and Charity*, 27) For present purposes it is important that sin be recognized as a fact of man's history and a part of the context in which the work of the New Adam has to be studied.

Man in Sin

To illumine the doctrine of the redemption, the theologian must get down to the specific details of the condition of man in sin and measure as exactly as possible its impact on him both as to nature and extent. This information will be relevant in examining the saving work of the Man of the last age, Jesus Christ.

There are some basic disagreements among Christians about the nature and effects of original sin. The gnostic identification of sin with matter—the creature of an essentially evil principle—would require that sin be described as a positive physical entity. The identification of sin with the devil leads to the conclusion that the devil dwells in the soul of the sinner. Luther and Calvin identified original sin with the inclination to personal sin experienced by everyone. Ordinarily called concupiscence, this inclination is offered as evidence of a thoroughgoing corruption of man, making him incapable of thinking or willing any moral good. Significantly, both Luther and Calvin taught that this condition of corruption is unalterable. When the sinner is set aright with God, or justified, no change takes place within him. His sin remains but God chooses not to impute it to him, regarding him as clothed with the merits of Christ.

The Church took issue with this Protestant explanation and in the Council of Trent offered a realistic but milder description of man in sin. (Cf. *The Life of Grace* in this series.) The identification of sin with concupiscence was rejected; concupiscence is an effect of original sin and leads to personal sin, but is not itself sin. Neither is man's sinful condition unalterable. Baptism removes all elements of sin from the soul of the sinner. (D792) The intellect and will of man are weakened by his sinful condition but remain essentially intact, making it possible for the sinner to engage in activity that is not sinful. (D814f) In short the Church denied the essential corruption of man as a result of original sin. Theologians ordinarily summarize the damages done to all men by Adam's sin as the loss of the supernatural and preternatural gifts and the weakening of the powers of human nature. This global treatment may be unfortunate. Undoubtedly the most critical privation is that of sanctifying grace, the essential element of original sin according to most theologians.

Within the framework of this summary, the theologian who studies the redemptive work of Christ can consider other, more personal aspects of sin and its impact on man. To these aspects of sin will correspond aspects and effects of the saving acts of Christ. Beginning with the fact that sin is a rejection of the love God bears us, the study of man in sin leads to the consideration of the changes worked in man by sin which result in his estrangement from God.

SIN A PERSONAL OFFENSE AGAINST GOD'S LOVE The Church teaches that the first man disobeyed a divine command and that this act was offensive to God. (D788f, 3018) The Genesis narrative describes the sin of Adam in terms of disobedience to a divine command. (Gn 3,1–6) Basic to the external act was an inner spirit of rebellion against the supremacy of God: Adam and Eve were moved by the desire to "be as gods." (Gn 3,5) Here lies the essence of their act; in this challenge to the dominion of God, expressed externally in the act of disobedience, can be seen the personal nature of their offense.

The rebellious character of every sin is evident in the descriptions of the sin of Cain (Gn 4,9f), and of the sins preceding the deluge. (Gn 6,5ff) Sinners are said to have provoked and angered God (Dt 32,21), to have rebelled against him (Ps 106[107],11), to have despised him. (Is 1,2) Jeremia compares the sinful people Israel to an unfaithful wife who has wronged her husband by many infidelities. (Jer 3,1–5; 31,22; cf. Os 1,2; Ez 16,35–38.) While there can be no question of man's sin effecting a change in God or disturbing the divine transcendence (Job 35,5–8), it is clear that sin by its nature is directed against God, is an evil before God and inevitably a personal offense to him. (D1290) The Church prays in this vein in the collects for the Thursday after Ash Wednesday and the feast of St. Bruno, October 6.

This fundamental notion of the sinful act is significant in understanding the permanent condition of the man who has sinned. This condition is verified in all who inherit sin from Adam as well as in those who commit serious personal sin. The act of sin effects a change in the sinner, he becomes different from what he had been before the sin. The first obvious effect of a sin against God is that the sinner is estranged from him.

THE SINNER AN "ENEMY OF GOD" This view of the sinner is found in the teaching of the Council of Trent, where it is said that Adam incurred "the wrath and indignation of God" (D788), that all men are "by nature sons of wrath" (Eph 2,3) as a result of Adam's sin (D793), and that sin alienates man from God (D797), making him an enemy of God. (D799) The quality of this estrangement can be seen in the Genesis account of Adam's sin. Before the sin, the man is pictured on familiar terms with God; after the sin, before any punishment is formally imposed, he hides himself from the presence of God. (Gn 3,8ff)

The parable of the prodigal son (Lk 15,11–32) illustrates the fact that the sinner "departs" from God. In it the son takes his share of the family property and goes "into a far country" to live independently of his father. (Lk 15,12f) The great saddening effect that this has upon the father becomes evident through his intense joy upon the son's return. The departure of the son, clearly an offense against his father, may be taken as illustrative of the sinner's offense against God.

Another aspect of this effect of sin can be seen in the scriptural references to God's reaction to man's offense. In the Old Testament

God is said to be angry and saddened by man's sin; he complains about the sinner or intervenes to avenge the injury done to his name. St. Paul speaks of the divine anger as turned on the sinner: "For the wrath of God is revealed from heaven against all ungodliness and wickedness." (Rom 1,18) All men in sin are called "sons of wrath" (Eph 2,3), and Paul speaks explicitly of sinners as inimical to God: "You yourselves were at one time estranged and enemies in mind through your evil works." (Col 1,21; Rom 5,10f; cf. Eph 2,13–16.)

This estrangement can be seen in the structure of sin itself. Theologians speak of sin as an "aversion from God and turning to a creature." St. Thomas includes "apostasy from God" as part of the explanation of every sin. (*S.Th.*, 1^a2^{ae},84,2 ad 2) This apostasy can be understood only in terms of an enmity between God and man and, as man is forced to speak of it, the displeasure of God with man.

Since this wrath cannot be understood as an interruption of God's love for man, the explanation must be sought in some change worked in man by sin. This change is found in man's loss of the life of grace, a loss that is referred to as the death of the soul.

SIN AS THE DEATH OF THE SOUL The Church referred at Orange and Trent to "sin, the death of the soul." (D175, 789) The life lost by the sinner is that of sanctifying grace, obviously not his human life. Grace can be described as a supernature enabling man to engage in activity beyond his ordinary human capacities during life, and then in beatific activity in heaven. The ability of man in grace to perform acts that are proper to God leads to the conclusion that elevating grace gives man a special likeness to God. He is said to participate in the divine nature or to be "deiform" by reason of it. The graced man can be said to be the adopted son of God since he can engage in activity analogous to that of the natural Son of God. Man has no access to this grace except by way of a gift from God; no merely human effort on his part can earn this supernatural life.

The life of grace can be taken as the foundation of man's friendship with God. Adorned with it, man is both God's friend and a member of his household. (D803, 799) Since there is a certain community of life between God and man in grace, there is a basis for the mutual love called friendship. Once man has lost this life, the basis for friendship is removed. Man becomes incapable of the supernatural love of God. (*S.Th.*, 2^a2^{ae},23,1)

St. Paul is quite plain about the lethal effect of sin: "And you, when you were dead by reason of your offenses and sins. . . ." (Eph 2,1) When speaking of Adam's sin, he indicates that death resulted from it: "Therefore, as through one man sin entered into the world and through sin death, and thus death has passed to all men because all have sinned. . . ." (Rom 5,12) In this context "death" has a multiple meaning: first, the loss of the gift of immortality, that is, the liability of men to physical death; second, the death of the soul; finally, the ultimate death of hell, should a man ratify Adam's sin with personal sin and end his natural life in that condition. Thus may the loss inflicted on man by sin be summed up.

The death of the soul renders man incapable of seeing God face to face and of doing anything that would help him achieve this destiny. It also destroys the basis of his friendship with God. Since there is no community of life, there can be no mutual love and hence no real friendship. Here lies the explanation of the wrath of God. His love for man in sin is not broken off but continues to be expended on man. The change in man, however, changes the effect this love has on him. Man without sin is free to receive the life of grace. Thus enlivened supernaturally, he can and does respond to God's love with a corresponding love—"supernatural charity" as theology terms it. When man destroys the life of grace by sin he becomes incapable not only of returning God's love but even of receiving it as his friend. Man in sin is no longer God's friend because he has made himself incapable of this friendship. Paradoxically, he can be called the object of God's wrath despite the fact that God's love for him is constant. The correction of this situation evidently does not involve any change in God, but in man. Repentance opens the sinner once again to the receipt of grace (though repentance itself is a result of grace). Repentance makes it possible for man to resume his friendship with God in the exchange of love.

SIN AS SLAVERY TO SATAN The turning of man from God and the consequent loss of his friendship has another sinister effect—man becomes a slave of the devil. This fact is stated explicitly by the Church: *man is enslaved to Satan as a result of original sin* (D788, 793), *and also of personal sin.* (D894) This view of sin, although not always well understood, has been prominent in Christian tradition. The devil was the instigator of the first sin (Jn 8,44) and continues to be "the adversary" inciting men to rebellion against God. (Jb 1,6–12; 2,1–7) He is called the "prince of this world" (Jn 12,31; 14,30; 16,11) and even the "god of this world." (2 Cor 4,4) Men in sin walk "according to the prince of the power of the air about us, the prince of the spirit which now works on the unbelievers." (Eph 2,2) The whole world after the sin of Adam is pictured as "in the power of the evil one." (1 Jn 5,19) Phrases like these convey the idea that, in some sense, man in sin lies subject to the devil's power.

St. Thomas explains man's subjection to the devil as a usurpation of dominion by the devil which is permitted by God. Man's sin involves withdrawal from God and a submission to the devil's suggestion, a usurpation of power since this action is grounded in deceit. He does not acquire real rights over man but seizes power treacherously and unjustly. God permits this usurpation and punishes man for submitting to it—or sinning. It may be said that he turns man over to the devil as an instrument of punishment. (*S.Th.*, 3,48,4 ad 2)

Man's enslavement to the devil implies other forms of bondage. St. Paul envisions man as "sold into the power of sin" (Rom 7,14), as a "prisoner to the law of sin." (Rom 7,23) Man in sin is a prisoner of the flesh, and "the wisdom of the flesh is hostile to God." (Rom 8,3–8) Subjection to death results from the sin of Adam. (Rom 5,12–17) The body of man in sin is "this body doomed to death" (Rom 7,24); because of sin, man is subject to physical death and the death of eternal damnation. This enslavement to sin, the flesh, and death may described as various ways in which the devil is permitted to exercise and manifest his dominion over man in sin.

The real involvement of Satan in the life of the sinner and Satan's implacable hostility to God constitute a vital aspect of the condition of man in sin. They lead to the expectation that the rescue of man from sin will involve a struggle with the devil.

THE DEBT OF THE SINNER TO GOD St. Anselm of Canterbury (d. 1109) developed what has been called the "legal aspect" of sin by teaching that any rational creature who does not give the submission of his every wish to God robs him of what is his due and thereby sins.

(*Why Did God Become Man?*, 11) Sin is thus regarded as an act of injustice, a personal injury given to God, since his rights over man are denied. The state of guilt which ensues involves the obligation of man to make restitution for the honor which he wilfully refused to God. For the remission of sin it is necessary that the sinner withdraw his will from the sin and make satisfaction to God for the debt owed or have the debt condoned. St. Thomas continued in this juridical vein a century later by teaching that an additional effect was man's liability to punishment for the offense given to God. (*S.Th.*, $1^{a}2^{ae}$,87,1)

The Work of the New Adam

On the supposition that the chief purpose God had in sending his Son was reparatory, we may take the fact of sin and its consequences as the point of departure for the saving work of the New Adam. Christ will bring his brothers back to God and restore them to their place in God's household. This is not to say that his saving work will be centered on man. Sin is a reality, but the changes it produces in the sinner result from the rejection of the love proffered by God. The saving work of the New Adam will first of all be objective, look to God, be centered on him. It is with this stage of the work of salvation that this study is concerned.

THE DIVINE INITIATIVE

Man Imprisoned by Sin

The Church is very firm about the helplessness of man in sin. Although the free wills of men were not destroyed by the sin of Adam, "so completely were they slaves of sin and under the power of the devil and of death, that neither the power of nature for the Gentiles nor the very letter of the Law of Moses for the Jews could bring liberation from that condition." (D793,811,790) This statement summarizes the thesis of St. Paul that neither nature nor the Law can be effective in liberating man from his sinful state. (Rom 1–3)

The fact that sin is fatal to the supernatural life of man leads to the conclusion that the sinner is impotent to release himself from the state of sin. With the loss of grace—the principle of supernatural activity—the very basis for any approach to God is lost. The natural acts of man have no value in setting aright his relation of special intimacy with God. From man's side the condition of sin is irreparable. (*S.Th.*, 1ª2ªᵉ,87,3)

Man's hope of recovery from sin is expressed in Psalm 50[51]. He has sinned against God (6–7), and he must therefore depend upon God to show him mercy and remit his sin. (3) God is called upon to sprinkle man and to wash him (9); to create in him a pure heart (12), to restore to him the joy of salvation (14), and to deliver him from the penalty of blood. (16) The implication is that the condition of the sinner is such that only God can extricate him from it; if there is to be salvation God must take the initiative.

God's Will to Save

God did take the initiative, "for he wishes all men to be saved and to come to the knowledge of the truth." (1 Tim 2,4) "What was impossible to the Law, in that it was helpless because of sinful nature, God has effected. By sending his Son in a nature like that of sinful man as a sin-offering, he has condemned sin within that very nature." (Rom 8,3) The sending of God's Son, born of a woman (Gal 4,4), was accomplished in the fullness of time, a climax of the divine plan "to bring all things into a unity in Christ." (Eph 1,10) Before this climax, in the centuries between Adam and Christ, the initiative of God was exercised in preparing all men for the salvation planned for them. During this period of preparation, "the mystery of his will" to save (Eph 1,9) was unfolded only gradually as God brought sinful man to religious and moral maturity.

This delay in bringing the plan of salvation to a climax obviously did not mean the reprobation of those who lived before Christ. Saving grace was available to all men and no one was condemned except for the deliberate refusal to use grace. This is implied in St. Paul's statement of God's will to save all men. After making the statement, Paul adds: "For there is one God and one mediator between God and man, himself man, Christ Jesus." (1 Tim 2,5) This addition reinforces the idea that God's will to save was genuinely universal, including all men of every era. The salvific will extends to all those for whom the one God is God and whose nature is shared by Jesus Christ. This includes every human being who ever has existed or will exist. The implication of 1 Timothy is that God's grace was available to all men living in the centuries between Adam and Christ. The same statement also implies that the graces given before Christ were given in view of his work as mediator. Christ's sacrifice had a retroactive effect since its values were available in the centuries before it was offered.

The Divine Plan

The first evidence of God's decision to inaugurate the rescue of man from sin is his pledge to set an adversary against the power of evil. (Gn 3,15) Another inkling of a plan to save all men emerges from God's agreement with Noa. (Gn 9,1–17) This pact between God and man lasted until man completed his desertion of God by the construction of the Tower of Babel. (Gn 11) These dimly realized, early gestures on God's part, as the sacred writers describe them to us, are significant in that they were initiated by God and included all men. They also show God's solicitude for the heathen since this promise and pact covered all mankind. Except for the statement that God took some pains that the gentiles should seek him, the details of his preparation of them for redemption are hidden. (Ac 17,26f) But that he did prepare them cannot be seriously challenged.

St. Paul dates the beginning of the history of salvation from God's call of Abraham and the promises made to him. God turned to a particular people, and from that point on the history of salvation is described in terms of God's relations with this people. These are "the Israelites, who have the adoption as sons, and the splendor of the divine presence and the covenants and the legislation and the temple worship and the promises; they have the patriarchs, and from them is the Messia according to natural descent, who is over all things, God [be] blessed forever." (Rom 9, 4f) The history of the Israelites is the history of salvation. In God's dealings with these people can be seen the lines of his plan for the salvation of all men.

THE PROMISE When God called Abraham he made several promises to him. (Gn 12) One of these had mysteriously wide horizons: "In you shall all the peoples of the earth be blessed." (Gn 12,3) This promise was the supremely important fact in the life of the Israelites and they looked to it for ever fuller and richer realizations, confident that God had prepared a gracious and secure future for them.

St. Paul was deeply conscious of God's promise to Israel and urged the Jews to recognize Christ as its perfect realization. (2 Cor 1,20) To this end, he presented the promise purified of popular but unworthy and inaccurate interpretations. This led him to stress two characteristics of the promise not usually adverted to by the Jews of his time.

The first can be called the *spirituality of the promise;* it was linked to God's free choice and man's free response, not to blood. While the promise had been made to Abraham and his descendants, it was not inherited by all the descendants of Abraham; it was received by Isaac to the exclusion of Ishmael, for example, and by Jacob to the exclusion of Esau. Paul's point was that the free choice of God determined the recipient of the promise. Its true heirs are the spiritual posterity of Abraham chosen by God. (Rom 9,6–13)

The second characteristic is the *universality of the promise.* Paul cited the text: "In you shall all the nations of the earth be blessed." (Gn 18,18) The principle of the universal extension of the promise is faith. Abraham had responded to God with faith and "it was credited to him as justice." (Gal 3,6) His true offspring, the rightful heirs of the promise, are those who imitate him in faith. (Gal 3,7ff) Paul's conclusion was that Christ and his work were the climactic realization of God's pledge of universal blessing, that the Christians united to Christ by faith were the spiritual posterity of Abraham and the true heirs of the promise.

It is relevant at this juncture to note that God was under no constraint in making the promise. It was not a reward for anything done by Abraham but a completely unilateral action on the part of God. The promise was made unconditionally and was based upon God's fidelity; it required nothing of the Israelites to insure its fulfillment. This was an immutable, eternally valid pledge of "blessing," the basic fact of God's relations with Israel and a critical point in the history of salvation.

LIBERATION FROM EGYPT AND THE COVENANT OF SINAI The initiative of God is evident also in the realizations of the promise. Outstanding among the instances of divine intervention in the history of Israel are the rescue of the Israelites from the slavery of Egypt (Ex 6), and the pact entered into by God and Israel on Mount Sinai. (Ex 19)

These two events are so closely related in the thinking of the Israelites that they are sometimes referred to as one. (Jer 31,32) To understand the character of the divine intervention, it is helpful to consider them together.

The detention of the Israelites in Egypt was truly a bondage for two reasons: first, because they were forced to give service to the Egyptians, and more significantly, because they were living in "a land of sin," distant from God and unable to offer sacrifice to him. (Ex 3,1; 5,1-12) The enslavement in Egypt came to be regarded as typical of the enslavement of man to sin. (Ez 20,5–9) Only God could effect their escape from this bondage. The divine efforts on behalf of Israel in slavery were called a work of salvation. More specifically, this work of salvation was described as a redemption of man or the payment of a ransom for him. (Ex 6,6; Dt 7,8)

The liberation of the Israelites was complemented by their pact with God. This pact was a bilateral one through the Lord's having declared the terms in which he committed himself to protect Israel in return for Israel's submission to him. (Ex 19–20) The significance lies in the fact that Israel became the people of God (Ex 6,6f); the nation was rendered holy, was consecrated to God, as a result of her covenant with him. (Ex 19,5f) Having been redeemed or ransomed from captivity by God, the Israelites became his possession by reason of their agreement with him. These were the two aspects, positive and negative, of the redeeming action of God in this particular fulfillment of the promise. This concept of redemption is meaningful in penetrating the nature and dimensions of the saving work of Christ.

The initiative of God in this whole redeeming work is apparent: "He has chosen you from all the nations on the face of the earth to be a people peculiarly his own. . . . It was because the Lord loved you and because of his fidelity to the oath he had sworn to your fathers that he brought you out with his strong hand from the place of slavery, and ransomed you from the hand of Pharao." (Dt 7,6ff) The covenant is sometimes described in the Bible in terms of a marriage contract. It is further noted that God took the first step in bringing the contract into being. (Ez 16,8)

Israël's part in the covenant called for observance of the Law given through Moses. But the people distorted the nature of the covenant and came to look upon it as a natural bond between God and themselves, which would indicate some sort of need for them on God's part. This led them to conclude that the hearing or possession of the Law was enough to make them just before God. Their infidelity to the Law did not disturb this sense of righteousness in them. Seen in this way, the Law proved to be more a barrier to friendship with God than a guiding light to it. The Law became an occasion for rebellion against God, and the sins of the Jews increased under the Law. St. Paul explained that God permitted this abundance of sin while keeping in mind the superabundance of grace to come. (Rom 5,20)

But the purpose of the Law was not completely frustrated. It proved to be a guardian of monotheism and of the divine revelations entrusted to Israel. It also insulated Israel from the greater excesses of the pagans. St. Paul sums up the success of the Mosaic ordinance: "Therefore the Law has been our tutor unto Christ, that we might be justified by faith." (Gal 3,24)

THE FREEDOM OF GOD

God's will to save all men, the plan of salvation, and the execution of the plan were always God's doing. This intervention in human history was not a reward of man's goodness or his fidelity to God, but a gift offered in the face of man's sinfulness. God was not responding to any obligation to man, for man in sin *has no rights* before God. Man was not exerting any pressure on God since grace, the only basis on which he could approach God, had been repudiated by his sin. The coming of the Second Adam to correct the sin of the first Adam and to provide new life and leadership to the human race resulted from God's initiative freely taken.

God's freedom in redeeming man has occasionally been questioned. Some have claimed that God was obliged by an internal necessity to restore man to his original condition. Others admit God's freedom to restore man, but maintain that, once decided, this restoration must be accomplished by the incarnation of the Son of God. Although the Church has never specifically rejected these opinions, they do contradict the theological tradition of Catholics and are incompatible with several relevant statements of the Church.

The prevailing theological tradition is summarized in the teaching of the local Council of Cologne (1860): God did not have to restore man to his original supernatural status but could have left him in the condition which he had chosen for himself. This tradition reflects accurately the mind of St. Paul who was emphatic about God's freedom in granting redemption: "They are justified freely by his grace" (Rom 3,24); "God, who is rich in mercy, was moved by the intense love with which he loved us, and when we were dead by reason of our sins, he brought us to life together with Christ." (Eph 2,4f) This emphasis on God's acting "freely" served to contradict Jewish claims to rights in the matter of salvation and was a flat rejection of the idea that God had to undertake the redemption of man. St. John clearly asserts the initiative of God and at the same time his freedom when he refers to the priority of divine love: "In this is the love, not that we have loved God, but that he has first loved us, and sent his Son as a propitiation for our sins." (1 Jn 4,10)

The Council of Trent did not make a special point of the divine freedom but did indicate that it is basic in the Church's thinking on redemption. A brief survey of God's redemptive plan mentions that "the heavenly Father, 'the Father of mercies and the God of all comfort' (2 Cor 1,3) sent Jesus Christ his Son to men." (D794) This passing reference to the "Father of mercies" cannot be fitted into a picture of God obliged to take up the work of redemption.

Although God did not have to see to man's redemption, it was fitting that he should do so. The inevitability of original sin as an inheritance makes it proper that God should show mercy to men who are not in the state of sin by their personal fault. The flexibility of man's will is another consideration. As long as man lives on earth, his will is not irrevocably committed either to good or to evil, but is changeable. It is fitting that God should give man the opportunity to turn back to him and resume the life he had lost. (S.C.G., 4,55)

Divine Love and Justice

The decision to rescue man from sin did not lead God into the necessity of doing it in any one way. God's love, goodness, and mercy could have been expressed in many ways. He could have simply condoned the offense; he could have required some penitential act by one man in the name of all; he could have required some penance from every man. Any act of glory given to his name would have been effective by his free decree.

God's decision as manifested in his plan was mysteriously rich and complex. Instead of calling for a nominal act of expiation—according to the Thomistic explanation—God made it possible for man to correct the imbalance caused by sin. Man could discharge fully the debt contracted by sin by making reparation equal to the offense given by sin. The divine plan called for giving to God honor that was at least as pleasing as sin had been hateful. (*S.Th.*, 3,48,2)

The decision to enable man to make perfect satisfaction determined the outline of the plan, in this view. Since sin is an offense against the infinite God, sin is "infinite" in this respect. No one man, however, nor even all men acting in concert, can give God infinite honor. The plan to make satisfaction for the offense of sin required expiation by man, since he is the sinner. This plan also called for the expiation to be made by one with infinite dignity, since the acts of anyone less would fall short of complete satisfaction. Thus the satisfaction of the requirements of justice (in the legal sense) was possible only to one who is at the same time God and man. (*S.Th.*, 3,1,2 ad 2)

These reasoned aspects of sin and satisfaction show the need of the incarnation of the Son of God to implement God's freely chosen plan of redemption. This is not to say that this explanation of the fittingness of the incarnation is complete. The redemption is a mystery of infinite love which escapes all of our attempts at analysis. Still, the reunion of God and man which takes place in the person of the incarnate Word, the healing of the breach between the two which means the reestablishment of their friendship, are all significant considerations in explaining the redemptive potential of the incarnation.

To keep the redemption in focus it is important to realize that the source and inspiration of the divine plan even in its juridical aspects, so called, were always the love and mercy of God. His love for man was the reason for the redemption, not one of its effects. Pardon for sin was subordinated to the redemptive acts of Christ. It was the love of God that provided that there should be redemptive acts. God responded to the sacrifice of Christ, but this sacrifice was part of God's plan and an effect of his love for man.

St. John's summary of the origin of the redemption cannot be surpassed: "For God so loved the world that he gave his only-begotten Son, that those who believe in him may not perish, but may have life everlasting." (Jn 3,16)

CHAPTER TWO

THE DIVINE REDEEMER

The next step in theological inquiry into the redemptive sacrifice of Christ is careful and complete identification of the New Adam. To understand the values and relevance of Christ's life and work for the correction of the situation of man in sin, it is important to establish with precision his identity and his potential for rescuing man from sin. These matters have been taken up to some extent in the volume in this series entitled

The Word Made Flesh. The present discussion is designed to explore those aspects of the identity of the Second Adam which are particularly cogent for understanding his redemptive activity. To this end, five subjects are taken up for examination: 1) the Word incarnate; 2) the instrument of the divinity; 3) the mediator between God and man; 4) the head of the human race; 5) the high priest. Each of these aspects of the identity of the New Adam will serve to show him capable of redeeming the human race.

THE WORD INCARNATE

The basic fact of the identity of the New Adam is that he is the second person of the Trinity "in habit found as a man." Eternally and unchangeably divine, in the fullness of time decreed by the Father he made his own an individual human nature to become a genuine and complete man. He is one with the Father and the Holy Spirit in that he is identified with the one divine nature; he is one with all men in that he possesses the same specific human nature with them. Nothing is subtracted from either nature by their union, nor do they mingle into something that is neither divine nor human. Both natures are integral and possessed by the same divine person, enabling this person to perform divine and human acts.

The ability of the Son of God to perform acts that are at the same time divine and human ("theandric") opens the way to some understanding of the redemption. Since he is man, he can and indeed must turn to the Father in submission, prayer, and sacrifice (*S.Th.*, 3,20,1; 21,1; 22,1); he can suffer and die to express his submission to the Father. (*S.Th.*, 3,14,1) These are acts done by a divine person who has a human nature. Since the doer of these acts is utterly sinless and a person who shares the glory of a Father who loved him from the beginning (cf. Jn 17,24), such acts will have a unique value. Any one of them will be more than acceptable to the Father, glorifying him more than all the good acts of all men taken together. This ability to give full submission to the Father and to render him fitting glory is basic to the God-man's effectiveness as the redeemer of all men.

THE INSTRUMENT OF THE DIVINITY

The redemptive significance of the human nature and the human acts of the Word incarnate are brought into better focus when it is seen that they are instruments used by the divinity to bring the redemption to completion. The impetus to redemption originated with the Father who sent his Son into the world to rescue man from sin. (Jn 3,16) As God, the Son was incapable of the activity freely called for by the divine plan of redemption, but by joining a human nature to the divinity in his person, he could do the things that were decreed for redemption. The human nature was the means by which the divine person could operate within the framework of the divine plan and effect the redemption as designed by the Father. This leads to the conclusion that the divine agent of redemption used his human nature as an instrument to produce the desired effect.

Because of its union with the divine substance in the person of the Word, the humanity of Christ should never be thought of as loosely and temporarily assumed by the divine person. This instrument is joined in a substantial unity with the agent using it. For this reason it is unique among the instruments used by God and is called the *conjoined instrument* of the divinity. (*S.Th.*, 3,2,6 ad 4)

The Church has not taught definitively that the human nature of Christ is an instrument united in substance to the divinity, but the Third Council of Constantinople (680–81) explained the distinction and the union of the divine and human wills in Christ in a way that strongly implies that the human nature and its powers are used by the divinity as an instrument. After stating that there are two wills in Christ, the council carefully established that there is no conflict between them: "And the two wills are not opposed . . . but the human will is compliant, and not opposing or contrary; as a matter of fact, it is even obedient to his divine and omnipotent will." (D291) The human will is the Word's own; it operates independently from the divine will but is always obedient to it. This is to say that Christ's human will and the nature of which it is part are used by the divine person to produce certain effects. The human nature can thus be recognized as an instrument of the divinity.

Certain divine activity—for example, creation—leaves no room for the use of an instrument. The human nature of Christ operates as an instrument of the divinity in an area determined by the purpose of the incarnation. This purpose was indicated at Constantinople: "There are two natural wills and operations concurring in harmony for the salvation of the human race." (D292) St. Thomas limits the power of the soul of Christ with the same principle: as an instrument of the Word, his human soul can effect all the miraculous changes in creatures that are related to the purpose of the incarnation. (*S.Th.*, 3,13,2) This purpose is the redemption of all men. The incarnation is essentially redemptive. The redemption should not be regarded as an episode in the life of the Word incarnate, but the work of his entire life on earth. The conclusion this points to is that all the activity of Christ, while essentially human, was controlled, directed, and used by God for the salvation of men.

The human nature of Christ was not an inert, unthinking tool moved about by that which was divine in him to produce the salvation of men. As an instrument it was used in a way proper to its nature; that is to say no violence was done to Christ in his rational or affective self. His human power of knowing and his freedom in willing were used by the Word who possessed them to bring about the desired effects. It is characteristic of a cause that is itself instrumental that its native qualities will be preserved and employed by the principal agent who wields the instrument. (*S.Th.*, 1,45,5)

On the other hand, the influence exerted by the divine person on the human nature is not to be regarded as an initial impetus applied from without by the principal agent. While the instrument is used according to its nature, it shares the movement and power of the agent employing it. The action of the principal agent elevates and makes its own the action of the instrument. The result is a single action, characterized by the use of the particular instrument but going beyond the proper power of the instrument. The principal agent is the responsible force in the action and the effect is determined by the power he is capable of and actually exerts. (*S.Th.*, 3,62,1) In all this, we may never reduce the human body and soul of Christ to the status of mere object or thing, since both together comprise the summit of free creaturehood before God.

Since the human nature of Christ is substantially and permanently united to his divine person, all the human acts of Christ are the acts of a divine person; they are used by the Word as instruments and are directed to the redemption of men. God in sending his Son is the principal and responsible agent of redemption, but this effect can only be achieved through the instrumentality chosen to bring it about, namely the free and conscious humanity that is supreme of its kind.

St. Thomas distinguishes two ways in which the human nature of Christ is used instrumentally by the person of the Word. The actions of this nature contribute to our salvation and cause grace in us insofar as some of them earned grace, and also because all of them are used by God as direct, efficient causes of grace in us. (*S.Th.*, 3,8,1 ad 1)[1]

Meritorious Cause of Redemption[2]

St. Thomas stresses the earning value of all that Christ did and suffered up to and including his death: Christ lived and died for all men that he might gain grace for them. He was circumcised for us that we might be spiritually circumcised (*S.Th.*, 3,37,3 ad 2); he was tempted for our sakes, that we might be helped against temptation. (*S.Th.*, 3,41,1) His death was the climax and summation of his meritorious activity. In view of his dying as he did, consciously and freely, man is liberated from sin. (*S.Th.*, 3,49,1) We shall have more to say later on the part Christ's glorification by the Father played in redeeming us.

The meritorious acts of Christ proceed immediately from his human nature and are aimed directly at honoring God. In all meritorious activity God establishes the framework within which merit is possible, wills the performance of the acts, and provides the means by which man can actually perform them. Thus, the acts of man can be thought of as ascending to God and at the same time producing in man a disposition which makes him deserving of the promised rewards. The principal

---

[1] Not all theologians agree that there is a real difference between the meritorious and efficient causality of Christ's human acts, e.g., P. Galtier, *De Incarnatione ac Redemptione* (Paris, 1947), pp. 340f. This disagreement is part of a debate about the order in which the instrumental causality of the human nature of Christ is to be located, i.e., whether in the moral, physical, or intentional order. Pursuit of the issues of this debate is impractical for the scope of this volume. For the purposes of this discussion, it will be assumed that the divine person, the Word, used the humanity in different ways.

[2] The meritorious value of Christ's activity will be taken up again in Chapter 5. The purpose of the present discussion is to underline the God-man's potential for accomplishing man's redemption.

agent of the meritorious acts of Christ is the divine person who performs the acts. These acts proceed from and bear the impress of the human nature. Their unique value is derived from the influence on that nature of the divine person whose nature it is. The Son of God in his human nature gives infinite glory to the Father. This activity produces in him (and consequently in all other men because of his solidarity with them) a title to a share in the glory of his Father. In view of his perfect obedience the Father communicates his glory to him. Christ's human nature and its activities, instruments of the divinity in the work of the redemption, are "justified," in the language of the New Testament. This vindication, which is an anointing or consecration, is a glorification of the human Jesus in which his brothers are free to share.

Efficient Cause of Redemption

If the meritorious cause looks first to God and produces its effects in man *indirectly,* the efficient causality should be thought of as descending from God and producing its effect in man *directly*. The effect carries the impress of the human instrument but is essentially determined by the divine agent.

The effect of the redemptive deed is the restoration of the life of grace. The initiative for the production of this effect is God's. In communicating grace to mankind, God uses the human nature of Christ as an instrument. Only the divine power can produce such an effect. In doing so, it elevates the action of the human nature utterly, producing the effect *through* and *with* the human action. There is no parallel in all nature to the divine instrumentality of the body and soul of the Savior.

All the acts of Christ are involved in this causality. All that he did, suffered, and received by way of reward, from his conception to his ascension, had the effect of producing man's salvation. This cause can be compared to a medicine prepared by a physician. The actual liberation of man from sin is effected only when this cause has been brought to bear on him, just as the cure of the sick man comes only with the application of the prepared remedy. Each event or mystery of the life of Christ modified and determined his human nature in such a way as to make this nature an apt instrument for the production of grace in man. These mysteries of Christ are events of the past, but the

Church does not think of them as completely in the past. They remain as stable dispositions of Christ's human nature, and as such exert an influence in the production of grace. The power of these events in the life of Christ is not limited by space or time. They become operative when man is brought into contact with the human nature of Christ as it now is in glory. (*S.Th.*, 3,56,1 ad 3)[3] This living contact is achieved through sacraments. Christ produces grace through sacraments, we say, yet at no time do we lose sight of the divine initiative, or of the fact that God is principal cause of the redemption.

THE MEDIATOR BETWEEN GOD AND MAN

Christ was not the first mediator between God and man. Various prophets, kings, and priests had been chosen by Yahweh to mediate between himself and Israel. Moses was particularly prominent, being the ambassador of God and the representative of the people in the making of the covenant of Sinai. (Dt 5,4) The function of each of these mediators was to serve as a bond between God and man, to reconcile them in time of enmity or to strengthen their union in time of amity. This function points up the role of the mediator—he stands between the two parties, distinct from each of them and at the same time having something in common with each. Moses was separated from the rest of his people to a degree that enabled him to represent God among them, yet he was sufficiently one of the people to represent them before God. From this position he could contribute to the pact between God and man.

The mediator was chosen for his task by God. If he was a prophet he was set apart by the coming upon him of the "word of the Lord." Priests and kings were anointed, a rite which placed them between God and man and made them eligible to represent one with the other. Christ was constituted mediator uniquely—through the incarnation. Godhead and manhood were united in his person. Since both were his possession, he was uniquely qualified for the role of mediator.

Pope Leo I underlined this fact. Emphasizing the integrity of the two natures in Christ and their union in the person of the Word, he

[3] The principle indicated here will be applied in Chapter 3 where the redeeming works of Christ are discussed.

makes this point: "Thus was lowliness assumed by majesty, weakness by power, mortality by eternity; a nature that could not be defiled was united to one that could undergo repayment of the debt attaching to our state. Hence as was suitable for the alleviation of our distress, one and the same mediator between God and man, himself man, Christ Jesus, was both mortal and immortal under different aspects." (D143)

St. Thomas, too, explains the mediatorial role of Christ on the basis of the union of the two natures. Christ is the mediator between God and man precisely as man. Regarded in his divine nature, Christ does not differ from the other divine persons in nature and power; there is no "distance" whatever between him and the Father and the Holy Spirit. Regarded in his human nature, he is "distant" from them. At the same time, he is superior to all other men and different from them because of the measure of his grace and glory.

Thus the God-man has the divine nature in common with the other divine persons, and his human nature in common with all men. He differs from the other divine persons because of the human nature, and from other men because of the divine nature. St. Thomas concludes that this position makes Christ competent to bring the gifts and commands of God to men and offer the prayers and satisfaction of men to God. (*S.Th.*, 3,26,2)

The significance of this fact for the redemption is obvious. Since the incarnation establishes Christ as the natural mediator between God and man, he is himself a substantial bond between God and man. Because both extremes are united in his person, this actual joining of God and man is the first stage of the renewal of all things in Christ. His mediatorial activity will bring the union to a more perfect stage and bring to an end the estrangement between God and man.

The official documents of the Church, strangely, do not feature the role of Christ as mediator. The Councils of Florence (1442) and Trent (1546) mention that redemption comes to us only through the merits of "the one mediator, our Lord Jesus Christ, who reconciled us to God in his blood" (D711, 790), but they scarcely do more. The notion is not further explored, probably because no heretical teaching challenged it. Nonetheless, these few references do serve to show that this aspect of Christ and his work is basic to the Church's thinking on the redemption. In her liturgies, the Church views Christ almost exclusively as mediator.

The inspiration of this thinking is St. Paul's clear statement: "For there is one God and one mediator between God and man, himself man, Christ Jesus who gave himself a ransom for all." (1 Tim 2,5f) This is Paul's only explicit mention of the point, but the theme of mediation runs through the epistles. Through the offices of Christ, man has grace (Rom 1,5), redemption (Rom 3,24), reconciliation (Rom 5,10f), peace (Rom 5,1); on the other hand, it is by Christ that man can exult in God. (Rom 5,11) The Epistle to the Hebrews presents Christ as mediator of the covenant, superior to Moses the mediator of the former covenant. (Heb 8,6; 9,15; 12,24) Christ's work is broadly outlined as a mediation between God and man: the enmity between God and man is resolved through the efforts of Christ, and the new pact between God and man is achieved through his mediation.

It is significant that emphasis is placed on the uniqueness of Christ's mediation. Among all the prophets, kings, and priests, he stands unrivalled. A sermon of Peter makes this point: "Neither is there salvation in any other. For there is no other name under heaven given to men by which we must be saved." (Ac 4,12) Some words of Christ in the fourth gospel are also pertinent: "I am the way, the truth, and the life. No one comes to the Father but through me." (Jn 14,6) Only Christ is the natural mediator between God and man, able to join man to God in himself in virtue of the eternal plan. Others can cooperate in this mediation (for example, Mary); they can act as agents of Christ, preparing men for redemption and salvation. These mediators before and after Christ are genuine enough, but their position and their work are inferior to Christ's and dependent on his. Only he is capable of the critical work of reconciliation. (*S.Th.*, 3,26,1)

THE HEAD OF THE HUMAN RACE

Christ's place as the representative of God among men can be seen in his unity with the Father in the divine nature and in his mission from the Father to be the agent of redemption. The explanation of his representation of men before God is more complex. This explanation must begin with the reality and integrity of his human nature. The fact that Christ is true man is the basis of his ability to mediate for men. But to mediate for all men and to be capable of working an effect in all, a mediator must be more than just another member of the human race. The role exercised by Christ implies that he has a position of power and influence in the race, that he is in some way linked with every other human being. The singular position that Christ possesses is evident from the description of him as Second Adam—he has been appointed the new head of humanity.

That Christ has such a predominant place in the human race can be derived from the picture of him as the bridegroom taking all humankind as his bride. (Jn 3,29; Mt 9,15; 22,2) Pope Leo XIII's comments on this picture are to the point: "When the eternal Son of God willed to assume the nature of man for the redemption and honor of man, and thereby to enter into a sort of mystical marriage with the entire human race, he did not do so before his chosen mother had given her free consent. She was in some way a representative of the human race." (Encyclical *Octobri Mense,* D1940a) Without exploring all the implications of this figure, it is apparent that Christ is seen in the closest relationship with all men since by the incarnation he has taken the entire human race as his own and has made himself one with it. Moreover, since Christ is the bridegroom, he is the dominant figure in the relationship; the human race as his bride is under his benign influence and power.

St. Paul is clear about the headship of Christ. He speaks of him as having "the primacy over every creature" (Col 1,15) and he spells out the superiority of Christ by adding: "All have been created through him and for him. He exists prior to all creatures, and in him they are all preserved in being." (Col 1,16f) Christ is not merely the best and noblest of creatures, he is the center of creation. Nor was this primacy usurped by Christ. It was decreed by God that he should have this first place, that through him he should reconcile all things to himself (Col 1,20), and that all things should be reestablished in Christ. (Eph 1,10)

This relationship between Christ, the New Adam, and the rest of men should not be taken to mean that Christ replaced Adam as the natural head of the race. Christ entered the race already established in its first father. He became a genuine member of the race, but not a "natural descendant," since his human nature resulted from the action of the Holy Spirit in the womb of his mother. (Lk 1,30–38) The headship of the human race assumed by Christ is therefore not in the order of nature but of a higher order. This means that while Adam remains the source of the natural life of all men, Christ has become the source of new life.

The explanation of the dominance of Christ as the supernatural head of the race leads into the discussion of the holiness of Christ. This holiness consists in the life that all men can or do derive from him.

Moral Holiness

The most obvious aspect of Christ's holiness is his sinlessness, which includes the incapability of sin. Christ did not contract original sin nor was his life marred by any personal moral fault. It is unthinkable that the Son of God should be stained by sin. While sin is a defect of the nature derived from Adam, Christ was not necessarily subject to all the usual defects of human nature. He freely assumed only those defects which were necessary and advantageous for his mission. That he did not choose to be burdened by sin is indicated from the manner of his conception which put him outside the normal line of human descent. This immunity from all sin, hereditary and personal, is singular to Christ and can be shared in by others only by way of special privilege. While it underlines the primacy of Christ among men, it is not by itself an explanation of his headship.

Substantial Holiness

Basic to the fact that Christ was without moral fault and that his human acts were always perfectly conformed to the divine will was his positive union with God by reason of what he was. His human nature was united to the divinity in a substantial union. The union by which the Word made this human nature his own could not fail to render it pleasing to God since it is brought into immediate and substantial contact with the uncreated holiness of the Word. Because the holiness of Christ's humanity results from the substantial union of the natures, it is called substantial holiness. This substantial holiness is uniquely Christ's. It cannot be shared by others and is not communicated by Christ to others.

Accidental Holiness

Distinct from substantial holiness is the holiness which results from grace. This holiness is called accidental because sanctifying grace is an accident in the soul which renders the creature like to God, making him capable of the beatific vision. It was lost for all men at the start, but reentered the world in the soul of Christ. St. John speaks of him at the beginning of his human existence as "full of grace and truth." (Jn 1,14) Leo XIII tries to convey an idea of the depth and extent of the graces of Christ: "In him resided the absolute fullness of grace in the . . . most efficacious manner possible; in him were all the treasures of wisdom and knowledge, charisms, virtues and every other gift." (Encyclical *Divinum Illud Munus,* "On the Holy Spirit," 9 May, 1897)

It is significant that while this fullness of grace enriched the soul of Christ, it was not a gift for himself alone. St. John points out that "of his fullness we have all received." (Jn 1,16) This means that Christ's fullness of grace was such that he could produce grace in the souls of others (as an instrument of divinity), and that the grace in the soul of Christ was the inexhaustible source of the life of all men. All are eligible to share in his fullness, to receive lifegiving grace from him, and thus to resume their place as adopted sons of God. This is the key to understanding the headship of Christ, that he is the source of supernatural life for all men.

Christ entered the world enriched by grace and capable of communicating it to others. But before this ability to share his fullness could be realized, it was necessary that the obstacle of man's offense to God be removed. When this block to the flow of grace was eliminated by the redemptive acts of Christ, it would be possible for men to join themselves to him, receive supernatural life from him, and begin to live this life in common with him.[4]

---

[4] To speak of Christ as the head of the human race is not to say that he is head of the mystical body. The difference can be seen in these words of Pius XII: "Although he had been constituted head of the whole human family in the womb of the Blessed Virgin, (he) exercises fully the office of head in his Church by the power of the cross." (Encyclical *Mystici Corporis,* "The Mystical Body of Christ," *AAS* 35 [1943], 206) Because Christ is the head of the whole race his fullness of grace *can* reach all men; it *does* reach those who, by faith and baptism, associate themselves with him and are thus incorporated into his mystical body.

Some insight into the headship of Christ can be gained by thinking of the supernatural life of all men as contained in Christ from the moment of the incarnation. The basis for this line of thought is found in the New Testament. St. Paul speaks of the Father choosing all men "in him" before the foundation of the world. (Eph 1,4) St. John is more explicit in his emphasis on the saving value of the incarnation itself. Salvation is an enlightenment of men with the Word who is the light taking possession of man and sharing his life with man. (Jn 17,3; 1 Jn 5,20) By the incarnation, the saving light-life enters the human race in the person of Christ. Whoever believes in Christ passes from darkness to light and from death to life. (Jn 3,36; 6,40) The incarnation, then, is central in the redemption because by it all men are mysteriously linked with Christ and are thus open to receive life through him. It should be noted that St. John fills out the picture of the redemption by indicating the necessity of Christ's redemptive acts for bringing the redemption to completion. (Jn 11,50ff; 1 Jn 4,10)

The theme of all mankind's being contained in Christ was brought to a high point by St. Irenaeus in the late second century. He speaks of Christ as summing up all men in himself. "When he became incarnate and was made man, he recapitulated in himself the long history of man, summing up and giving us salvation in order that we might receive again in Christ Jesus what we had lost in Adam, that is the image and likeness of God." (*Against Heresies,* 3,18,1) The key to this idea is that by the incarnation God is brought into contact with all men who are contained in Christ. God and man are thus rejoined in Christ and all flesh is in some way divinized, since all flesh is contained in Christ and is brought into contact with his divinity.

This doctrine of recapitulation is significant in the emphasis it gives to the oneness of the human race with Christ its head. It is striking in the clarity with which it outlines the basis of the properly redemptive activity of Christ, showing his ability to act in the name of all men and the eligibility of men to benefit from his acts. If it is taken to mean that the redemption was completed by the mere fact of incarnation, it is not in agreement with the clear statements of John and Paul that the death and resurrection of Christ are the decisive acts of redemption.

St. Thomas underscores the headship of Christ in his theology of redemption. In his explanation of the effects of Christ's merits, he emphasizes that Christ and all men form one mystical person. The benefits of the works of Christ, the head of this person, extend to all men because they are the members of the person. (*S.Th.*, 3,19,4) He makes the same point in speaking of the satisfactory value of Christ's works for all men. (*S.Th.*, 3,48,2 ad 1) In explaining the liberation of all men from sin by Christ, he compares his work to the operations within the natural body of man—the hand can expiate a fault committed by the foot. Since Christ is the head of all men, forming one person with them, his activity can liberate from sin all men who are the members of his body. (*S.Th.*, 3,49,1)

Recognition of this solidarity of Christ with every human being is necessary for an appreciation of his ability to redeem all men. If this oneness is granted, some penetration is made into the universal effectiveness of his redemptive acts. His mysterious contact with all men transcends time and space and makes it possible for all to share in the value of his work. The nature of his link with men, that is, that he is the source of supernatural life for them, also clarifies the meaning of his merit. It points to the importance of his resurrection in the divine plan, and opens the way to understanding the function of his mystical body and the sacraments in the realization of salvation for each one.

THE HIGH PRIEST

The nature of Christ's priesthood must be studied if his redemptive work is to be understood. This is the specific element of his mediation between God and man, establishing his ability to offer sacrifice to the Father and in this way to redeem all men. It must be pointed out how significant the priesthood of Christ is in the work of the incarnation. Many theologians explain the union of the two natures, or the "grace" of this union, in terms of the anointing of Christ the priest.

The Church has asserted the fact of Christ's priesthood firmly: "The divine Scripture says that Christ became the high priest and apostle of our praise (*confessio*), and offered himself up for us to God the Father in the odor of sweetness." (D122) [5] The purpose of this statement was

[5] This is the tenth of St. Cyril's "anathemas" against Nestorius. They are ordinarily associated with the Ecumenical Council of Ephesus (431) but never received conciliar approval and cannot be regarded as statements of the *solemn* teaching authority (*magisterium*). Their orthodoxy has never been questioned by the Church, however, and they have been influential in later formulations of doctrine. They can be regarded as statements of the *ordinary* teaching authority.

to contradict the Nestorian claim that the individual human person, Jesus, was a priest, but that the divine person in his human nature could not be called a priest.

The Council of Trent, in laying the foundation for the discussion of the institution of the sacrifice of the eucharist, made this statement by way of summarizing the Catholic tradition: "It was necessary according to the merciful ordination of God the Father that another priest arise according to the order of Melchisedech, our Lord Jesus Christ, who could perfect all who were to be sanctified and bring them to fulfillment." (D938)

The constant reference to Christ as a priest "according to the order of Melchisedech" in the Epistle to the Hebrews and in Christian tradition calls for some explanation of this mysterious figure in the sacred narrative. King of Salem and priest of "the most high god" (El Elyon), Melchisedech blessed Abraham and received tithes from him. (Gn 14,18ff) Since he was both king and priest, his was a royal priesthood. (Ps 109[110],1ff) His dominion over others is demonstrated by his blessing of Abraham, since such a blessing is a sign of authority. The universality of his dominion is indicated by Abraham's offering of tithes. Because Abraham was the depositary of the universal promise of God (Gn 12,3), it was argued by the author of Hebrews that the tithing constituted a universal submission to the royal priesthood of Melchisedech. (Heb 7; cf. *S.Th.*, 3,22,6.) Melchisedech is also presented in the Genesis account without any mention of ancestors or descendants, and no descriptions of his later days. He came to be regarded, therefore, as a timeless figure who did not receive his priesthood by carnal descent as did the Levites.

The implications of the description of Christ's priesthood as "according to the order of Melchisedech" revolve about the superiority of Christ's priesthood over the levitical priesthood, and of the new covenant negotiated through Christ over the covenant of the Old Law. Although the priestly office and the offering of sacrifice had always been characteristic of the relations of God and man, the priesthood and the priestly work of Christ transcend all that had gone before.

The first point of superiority in the priesthood of Christ is its royal character. Joined to his priestly powers was authority over his subjects and, very particularly, over the levitical priesthood. (Heb. 7,9) Nor was the ministry of Christ limited as was that of the Levites. The boundaries of their ministry did not go beyond Israel, while that of Christ extended to all men, holding promise for all and including all in its authority. Unlike the levitical priesthood which, as an institution, was temporary (Heb 7,11–14), the priesthood of Christ is forever. (Heb 7,17) While the priestly ministry of individual Levites ended with death; Christ, "because he continues forever, has an everlasting priesthood." (Heb 7,24) His priesthood is eternal, conferred on him by God and not inherited "according to the law of carnal commandment" (Heb 7,16), unchangeable, and not subject to death.

Another point of superiority in the priesthood of Christ is found in his holiness. The Levites, being sinners, were obliged to offer sacrifice for their sins; Christ, however, was without fault. (Heb 4,15; 7,26) He was always pleasing to God (Heb 7,25), offering him perfect obedience (Heb 5,7f) and fidelity. (Heb 3,2.6)[6] Looking to men who were the beneficiaries of his ministry, he showed a perfect compassion with them and in this way provided another indication of his moral perfection. (Heb 5,2; 2,17) This perfect holiness of the Lord Jesus is evidence of the singularity of his priesthood and is part of the explanation of his unique effectiveness in opening the way to God for all men.

The timelessness of Christ's priesthood and the transcendent holiness which characterize it are explained by the fact that he was constituted a priest by the incarnation. His priestly character dates from the first instant of his human existence. As has been pointed out, Christ was anointed, constituted a priest, by the "grace of union." Since the union of the natures is perpetual, it becomes quite evident that Christ the priest continues forever and "lives always to make intercession. . . ." (Heb 7,24f) Although his priesthood came into existence only with the beginning of his human life, the fact that this priest is also the eternal Son of God contributes to the notion of the timelessness of his priesthood. The very fact that he is both God and man is basic to the explanation of his perfect human holiness and the unique power of his priestly ministry.

Recognition of the link between the priesthood of Christ and the incarnation illumines the statement that the priesthood was conferred on him with an oath. (Ps 109[110],4) Like every priest, he was called

[6] A period between verse numbers indicates that the verses cited are successive but nonconsecutive.

to this dignity by God (Heb 5,4ff), and was not merely an agent chosen by men to represent them before God. Nor was he committed to his task by men. By reason of the incarnation he was immediately anointed and given his mission by the Father.

When it is realized that Christ became a priest when he became a man and that there was no moment of his human existence when he was not a priest (Heb 5,1; 10,5ff), another unique aspect of his priesthood emerges. This priesthood is not something that the Lord received as an addition to his human nature or an adornment. It is not a quality or power that came to him after he had begun his existence as a man. The implication is that, given the divine decree of the redemptive incarnation, the God-man was necessarily a priest. The Word incarnate would be unintelligible were he not a priest. His priesthood is not something that he received, as is the case with all other priests; it is something that he is. Christ is identified with his priesthood.

This fact makes it possible to put the ordained priest in perspective. St. Paul describes priests as "ministers of Christ and dispensers of the mysteries of God." (1 Cor 4,1) They share to some degree in the priesthood of Christ by receiving the character of holy orders. The priesthood is something received from Christ by an existing man which likens him to Christ, makes him capable of doing some of the things proper to the Lord, and places him, as a priest, in essential dependence on him.

The Epistle to the Hebrews describes the redemptive work of Christ precisely and at length as the work of a priest. He is "the apostle and high priest of our confession" (Heb 3,1; 4,14; 8,1; 10,21); because he is our high priest we have access to the Father (Heb 10,21); he is the "high priest of the good things to come" (Heb 9,11); as high priest he is the realization of the divine plan of salvation. (Heb 7,26) In becoming a member of the human race, Christ achieved a oneness with all men, was constituted a priest, and, further, shared in the weakness and temptations of his brothers "that he might become a merciful and faithful high priest before God to expiate the sins of the people." (Heb 2,17f)

The fact that Christ is a priest is important for assessing his stature among men, but, more to the purpose of this discussion, it provides an insight into the nature of the redemption. It can be expected that the work of the Second Adam will be that of a priest "that he may offer gifts and sacrifices for sins." (Heb 5,1)

CHAPTER THREE

THE WORKS OF THE REDEEMER

When the relations of the New Adam with his Father and with the human race are recognized, it becomes possible to examine what he did and suffered to accomplish the redemption. These acts of redemption are the realization of the potential of the redeemer. In this discussion, it is well to investigate the decisive acts of redemption in light of the fact that the human nature of Christ is the instrument of divinity. St. Thomas points out that because this is so, all that Christ does and suffers contributes to the salvation of men. These events or mysteries of Christ's time on earth contribute to the redemption precisely as instruments used by God. (*S.Th.*, 3,48,6; 49,1) As instrumental causes of the redemption, the various mysteries will produce their proper effects, each in a way determined by the nature of the mystery. All of them conspire to form the one perfect work of redemption.

It became more or less customary, from the end of the patristic period, to see the decisive acts of redemption in the Savior's passion and death. This has been regarded as the truly critical area of redemptive activity, while what preceded and followed has in the past been looked upon as meaningful, but not essential, to redemption. This explanation developed from a general although never universal tradition of emphasizing the legal aspects of the redemption. It was recognized that the sinner is in debt to God since his sin was a refusal to give due honor to the Creator; and since the sin was also a violation of the divine law, the sinner is liable to punishment. If this twofold obligation completely explains the situation of man in sin and his need for redemption, the death of Christ can be seen as the discharge of man's obligations and the totality of the redeeming work.

Such an explanation is supported by the statement of Trent that the gifts lost by Adam were regained and the satisfaction of the requirements of justice accomplished by "the most holy passion on the wood of the cross." (D799) This statement was made with concern for the Protestant denial of man's ability to do anything positive to contribute to his own salvation. It looked to the redeeming work of Christ exclusively in terms of the meritorious and satisfactory values of that work, and of man's participation in it sacramentally. The discussions of theologians have until recently centered largely on this text of Trent, and have concentrated on references to the Scriptures and St. Thomas which deal with the saving power of the death of Christ. These discussions have contributed substantially to the understanding of the redemption. There can be no quarrel with the validity of the basic thesis that men are saved by the death of Christ. But the completeness of this thesis is open to challenge, and theologians have become more and more preoccupied with the redemptive value of the other mysteries of Christ's time on earth (his redemptive hour, *ōra;* season, *kaíros*). They have tried to establish with exactness the contribution of each of the mysteries of Christ and to sketch out the complete pattern of the work of redemption.

This theological effort is warranted by the fact that the Church has always prayed for the fruits of redemption with an eye to mysteries other than the death of Christ: "O God, whose only-begotten Son, by his life, death, and resurrection has obtained for us the rewards of eternal salvation. . . ." (Collect, Feast of the Most Holy Rosary) Immediately after the words of consecration in the Roman liturgy, again seeking the application of the values of Christ's saving work, the Church prays: ". . . calling to mind the blessed passion of the same Christ, your Son, our Lord, his resurrection from hell, and also his glorious ascension into heaven. . . ." St. Thomas, too, broadens the basis of the redemptive acts of the Lord in his discussions of the instrumental causality of Christ's human nature.

The aim of this chapter is to discuss the values and decisive character of all the acts of Christ. Attention is given to the life, teaching, and death of Christ. But inevitably, because of the present state of the question, particular emphasis is given to the causality achieved by his resurrection and ascension.

THE LIFE OF CHRIST

The Epistle to the Hebrews dates the beginning of the priestly mediation of Christ from the first moment of the incarnation: "Therefore in coming into the world, he says, Sacrifice and oblation you would not have, but a body you have fitted to me; in holocausts and sin offerings you have had no pleasure. Then said I, Behold I come . . . to do your will, O God." (Heb 10,5ff) The clear implication of these words is that every instant of Christ's human existence was spent in the effort to redeem men from sin. The will of the Father is that all men should be saved through the mediation of Christ. Jesus is pictured at the beginning of his human life, still in the womb of his mother, committing himself to the execution of that will. This is his first human act, and it is directed to redemption. These words can be said to enunciate the theme of the life of Christ. They express the idea that his execution of the Father's will to save continued uninterrupted.

The meritorious value of Christ's activity up to and including his death can be known from the goodness of all his acts. (Jn 8,29) The degree of merit can be gauged from the perfect human holiness of Christ and from the fact that his human acts are those of the Son of God. Every act of Christ was aimed at the salvation of men and contributed to that end because of its meritorious value. (*S.Th.*, 3,37,3 ad 2; 39,1; 41,1) Although the infinite value of any one of his acts is sufficient to earn the redemption of all men, the Father willed that the meritorious value of all of Christ's acts should be summarized in his passion and death. It is from that mystery of Christ, therefore, that account is taken of all his meritorious acts; each act of Christ's life did contribute, however, to the total value of his merit, and so each is an instrumental cause of redemption.

The acts of Christ's life previous to the Paschal mystery contributed to redemption by way of efficient causality also. We have already pointed out that in the faith of the Church the events of Christ's life are not completely in the past. Each event of Christ's earthly stay should be regarded as a factor which modified and determined his human nature in a way to make this nature an apt instrument for the production of grace in man. In this sense, all the mysteries of Christ's life contribute to the formation of the remedy for sin. More than that, they endure in his human nature, and become operative and productive of specific graces when man comes into contact with them. Pius XII points out that the mysteries of Christ "are ever present and active." Not only are they examples of perfection, we are told, they are "sources of divine grace," "and they still influence us because each mystery brings its own special grace for our salvation." (Encyclical *Mediator Dei,* "On the Sacred Liturgy," D2297) Thus every event in the life of Christ should be regarded as an instrument of God's will to save, and directly contributory to the total effect of redemption.

THE TEACHING OF CHRIST

Quite apart from the considerations just mentioned, the teaching of Christ made a distinct contribution to the redemption. This teaching was the discharge of his prophetical office and was a vital part of his mediation between God and man. (Heb 1,1f; Is 61,1; Lk 4,16–21) As a true emissary from the Father, he is "teacher and lord" (Jn 13,13);

he is the *only* teacher (Mt 23,10), "the light of the world" (Jn 8,12), and "the way, the truth and the life." (Jn 14,6)

Christ's superiority over other teachers and the special significance of his message are part of the pattern of redemption. He is the eye-witness of the heavenly doctrine he preaches (Jn 3,11); he relays to men truths he received from the Father. (Jn 7,16) His access to this truth is ascribed to his unique relationship to his Father. He can reveal the Father because he is "the only-begotten, who is in the bosom of the Father." (Jn 1,18) Since he is the Son, he and the Father have a complete knowledge one of another. This knowledge is his by right, but he shares it with those to whom he preaches. (Mt 11,27; Jn 6,46)

Nor is the teaching of Christ simply a matter of presenting a series of propositions to his listeners. He is both the natural Son of God and a revelation of the Father, "being the brightness of his glory and the image of his substance." (Heb 1,3) He is "the power of God and the wisdom of God" (1 Cor 1,24) and "has become for us God-given wisdom." (1 Cor 1,30) The believer in Christ comes into contact with Christ himself and also with the Father who sent him. (Jn 12,45) Christ is the object of faith. St. Paul speaks of his own preaching not as the presentation of truths made known by Christ, but as the presentation of "Christ and him crucified." (1 Cor 2,2)

In presenting himself as the object of faith Christ made a vital contribution to the fact of the redemption, namely his own teaching. He corrected the common distortions of the images of God and man and thus disposed his followers for the redemption. The restoration of God to the center of man's thinking, the replacement of fear of God in the popular mind with love for him, the establishment of the value and dignity of the individual, all helped prepare men to recognize and appreciate the work of redemption. But, most significantly, his teaching brought men to belief in himself, which meant living contact with the redeemer and redemption. To believers was given "power of becoming sons of God." (Jn 1,12) Belief in Christ enabled men to identify themselves with Christ, share in his life, and become eligible to enjoy with him the good pleasure of the Father. Belief in Christ, then, even before the mystery of salvation was accomplished, comprised the beginning of salvation and the first stage in the enjoyment of eternal life. (Jn 20,31; 1 Jn 1,1–4) This initial part of the saving design of the Father, and all Christ's words spoken "for us and our salvation," prepared the way for the acceptance in faith of the mystery by which we are saved.

THE DEATH OF CHRIST

While every action of Christ's life had a saving purpose and value, the actions most obviously decisive for redemption are contained in his passion and death. This was stated firmly at Trent (D799, 940) and is reflected in the prayer of the Church. In one of the prayers before communion, the priest addresses Christ "who, according to the will of the Father, did by your death . . . give life to the world." The Church sings its gratitude to God "who did establish the salvation of the human race on the tree of the cross." (Preface of the Holy Cross) Both prayers, it should be noted, originated in the medieval period, when insistence on the near-exclusive saving character of Calvary was at a high point; they nonetheless express the true faith of the Church.

These statements reflect the mind of St. Paul on the redemptive value of Christ's death. Paul strikingly ascribes the redemption to the blood of Christ: we are justified by his blood (Rom 5,9); the blood of the cross has reconciled all things to God the Father (Col 1,20); "in him we have redemption through his blood." (Eph 1,7) St. Peter's first epistle, too, states the saving value of Christ's death: "Because Christ also died once for sins . . . that he might bring us to God." (1 Pt 3,18)

This brief presentation of the fact that Christ's death is a cause of the redemption is in no sense complete. The texts cited are only a sampling of the available evidence. The limited purpose of these lines is to establish the basic fact that the death of Christ was one of the basic elements in his work of redemption. The discussion of the sacrifice of Christ in Chapter 4 and the effects of the sacrifice in Chapter 5 will be concerned largely with Christ's death.

Christ's Voluntary Death

If Christ's death is to be kept in perspective as the carrying out of the will of the Father that he should redeem man, and as the instrument of redemption chosen by the Father (or by Christ, since both theories are put forward), it becomes important to realize that death was not forced on Christ against his will. The formation of the plot against him, his arrest, trial, conviction, and execution were the visible dimensions of his last days. Beneath these events and giving direction to them was the divine plan. Every detail of the passion and death of Christ was a part of the Father's design of redemption, implementing his will to save all men. There were no unplanned circumstances or surprising developments in the agony and death of Christ. All bore a relation to the details of the fourth Servant Song in the book of Isaia. (Is 53) It is also evident from the synoptic gospels that Christ knew beforehand the details of the passion and the way in which he would die. (Mt 16,21; Mk 9,30; 12,1–12)

The foreknowledge of Jesus points up the fact that he freely accepted the Father's will and deliberately committed himself to its execution. (Jn 10,17f) It would appear that he had been overpowered by his enemies, but he made it clear that he had the resources to resist them had he willed to do so. (Mt 26,53) He had demonstrated his powers before (Jn 18,6); that he did not use them at the time of his passion is indicative of his complete freedom in accepting the will of his Father. (*S.Th.*, 3,47,1)

Christ's Obedience

The freedom of Christ in accepting the divine pattern of redemption underlines the fact that in submitting to this passion and death he was being obedient. There are explicit references to a command he received from his Father. (Jn 10,18; 14,31) There is a clear expression of his obedience to the Father's command despite his agonizing vision of its consequences for him. (Lk 22,42) This obedience was expressed again in his docile surrender to the men who had come to arrest him. (Jn 18,4–11) Finally, he signaled the completion of the work prescribed by the last words attributed to him. (Jn 19,28ff)

Christ's obedience was considered by St. Paul to be the critical element of his redemptive acts. Paul contrasts Christ's obedience with Adam's disobedience, and presents this as a basic factor in the corrective work of the Second Adam. (Rom 5,19; cf. *S.Th.*, 3,47,2.) Paul also emphasizes this obedience in his brief analysis of Christ's humility: "He humbled himself, becoming obedient to death, even to death on a cross."

(Phil 2,8) These statements, which result from Paul's theological penetration into Christ's death, provide a view into the inner spirit of the sufferings of Christ.

Given the extent and the depth of the sufferings of Christ (cf. *S.Th.*, 3,46,5–7), the command of the Father committing him to the crucifixion, if there was such an explicit command, presents a problem to the theologian. Can this in any sense be evidence of a hatred for Christ by his Father? Some have thought so, maintaining that since Christ was burdened with the guilt of all men he became in some way hateful to his Father. This explanation is not acceptable. It would involve an impossible transfer of real guilt to an innocent party, not to speak of leaving unexplained the explicit references to Christ as "holy, innocent, undefiled, set apart from sinners." (Heb 7,26) It should be kept clear that Christ did not assume the guilt of sin, but the obligation of making satisfaction for the sins of all men. Nor was his Father's love for him at any time interrupted or diminished. *The Father's command to achieve the redemption* (including the command to die, in the view of some theologians) *should be seen in relation to the unparalleled glorification of Christ which resulted from it* (Phil 2,9; Is 9,6), *and to the salvation of all men.* (Jn 3,16) Thus the Father's command was prompted not by hatred but by love for Christ and for the human race. (Jn 10,17f; 1 Jn 4,10; cf. *S.Th.*, 1,20,4 ad 1.)

The possibility of interpreting the Father's command as an act of cruelty may come to mind. This notion can be rejected out of hand as incompatible with divinity. But quite apart from this consideration, it should be recognized that the Father's infinite love for all men was shared by Christ. The Father's command was prompted by this love. Christ's free submission to the command was an expression of his perfectly attuned love for men. Christ was not an unwilling or reluctant tool of divine mercy for others but a free, instrumental agent, deliberately engaging in the acts that were decisive for redemption. (*S.Th.*, 3,47, 3 ad 1) In view of these facts, the "command" to die on the cross cannot be construed as cruel. Judas, the Jewish leaders, Pilate and his Roman functionaries, also figured in the death of Christ, but unlike the Father they acted from greed, envy, and fear. (*S.Th.*, 3,47,3 and ad 3) Christ did not share in their mind and spirit. Their acts were criminal, not intended by God, but only permitted. (*S.Th.*, 3,47,6 and ad 3)

Christ's Love

The roots of Christ's willingness to suffer as an instrument of divine mercy for the salvation of all men are in his love. His love for his Father prompted his ungrudging and unhesitating submission to the divine plan of redemption. His love for men is expressed in the parable of the good shepherd who lays down his life for his sheep. (Jn 10,15) This love is such that it moves him to surrender his life for his friends (Jn 15,13), and from this giving of his life for all men it is possible to know the full measure of his love. (1 Jn 3,16) The heart of Christ is singled out for special devotion by the Church precisely because it is the symbol of his love for his Father and for all men. (Pius XII, Encyclical *Haurietis Aquas,* "On the Sacred Heart," *AAS,* 48 [1956], 316f) The Church prays thus concerning the Sacred Heart: "that from his opened heart, as from a sanctuary of divine bounty, might be poured out upon us streams of mercy and grace; and that in his heart, always burning with love for us, the devout may find a haven of rest and the penitent a refuge of salvation." (Preface of the Sacred Heart)

The Death of Christ as an Instrument

Christ's freely given obedience and love are the basis for the moral value of his passion and death. His painful dying had meaning and value only because it expressed these inner sentiments. Because of this interior spirit, the dying of Christ can be seen as an act of religion, pleasing to the Father, and thereby profitable or meritorious for all men. Thus did the divinity use all the resources of the human nature of Christ to effect the redemption by way of meritorious causality.

Like the other mysteries of Christ's life, his death was used also as an efficient instrumental cause of redemption. In this connection, St. Thomas distinguishes between the dying of Christ which was meritorious and the fact of his death, or the state of separation of soul from body, which contributed to the redemption as an instrument of efficient causality. The proper redemptive effect of the death of Christ is also specified by St. Thomas. Citing Romans 4,25, he argues that the death of Christ results in the destruction or removal of sin which is the death of the soul; it will also offset the death of the body, and thus play a part in the ultimate victory of man. (*S.Th.*, 3,50,6) The completion of this work, by bringing man to supernatural life and then to final glorification, is the proper effect of the resurrection of Christ and will be discussed in the next section.

THE RESURRECTION OF CHRIST

Christ's resurrection has often been regarded as something of an epilogue to his passion and death: a personal vindication of Christ, a basis for faith in him, a pattern for man's rising from sin and ultimately from death. In the authentic tradition, the resurrection of Christ is given a much more meaningful position in the plan and execution of redemption. The resurrection is recognized as a co-cause—with the death of Christ—of man's redemption. Both of these mysteries are used as instruments of the divinity, each of them contributing in its own way to the total effect. The purpose of this discussion is to establish the fact of the causality of the resurrection and to indicate the proper effect of the resurrection in the redemption. A more extended discussion of the manner in which this causality is exerted will be taken up in Chapters 4 and 5.

The Synoptics

The place of the resurrection of Christ is not clearly outlined in the Gospels of Matthew, Mark, and Luke. The first prominent theme of these documents is the coming of the kingdom. "The time is fulfilled and the kingdom of God is at hand. Repent and believe in the gospel." (Mk 1,15) Christ is described as the herald of the kingdom and the leader of the people. A new theme is introduced with the teaching of the coming death of Christ. Christ has come "to give his life as a ransom for many." (Mt 20,28; Mk 10,45) This death is seen as a part of the divine plan of redemption. A third theme is introduced which serves to join the other two. The resurrection of Christ is also a part of the divine plan. "From that time, Jesus began to show his disciples that he must . . . be put to death and on the third day rise again." (Mt 16,21; Lk 24,46) The link between the death of Christ and his resurrection is seen in the statement: "Did not Christ have to suffer these things before entering into his glory?" (Lk 24,26) The implication is that death, and precisely death on the cross, was a preliminary condition for Christ's entrance into glory.

These considerations lead to several conclusions. The coming of the kingdom is realized with the resurrection of Christ. This inauguration of the promised kingdom with the glorification of Christ underlines the importance of the resurrection. In the divine plan, the resurrection follows necessarily upon the death of Christ. While this link between the resurrection and the death of Christ is clear enough to recognize, the synoptics leave it unexplained. The death of Christ is described as "the ransom for many" (Mt 20,28), but the resurrection is simply stated as a fact without any explanation of its precise function in the redemptive plan.

St. John

At times, St. John seems to attribute redemption to the fact of the incarnation without reference to the redemptive activity of Christ. But the full statement of this theme includes the fact that the incarnation does not become effective for redemption until the glorification of Christ. At that time, saving faith in Christ becomes a factor in the achievement of everlasting life. (Jn 3,14f) To fulfill his redemptive mission, Christ prays to the Father for glorification; with this glorification, he will be able to give eternal life to all. (Jn 17,1f) The eternal life which Christ confers is knowledge of the Father and of Christ himself, sent by the Father. Once Christ is glorified, this knowledge will become operative for the salvation of his disciples and for all who will believe in him. The final result will be the union of all those saved with Christ and the Father, and the sharing of all these men with Christ in the glory of the Father. (Jn 17,3–26)

This cursory glance at John shows the resurrection as a vital factor in the redemptive work of Christ. But the precise nature of the effect of the resurrection is still not brought into focus.

St. Paul

In the theology of St. Paul, the resurrection of Christ, together with his death, is a major cause of the redemption. Defending himself against Agrippa, Paul maintained that he was testifying to what the prophets and Moses said would come to pass, namely "that Christ was to suffer, that he first by resurrection from the dead was to proclaim light to the people and to the Gentiles." (Ac 26,22f) The prominence given to the resurrection of Christ in the divine plan of redemption is brought into sharper focus in Paul's insistence on the doctrine of the general resurrection. To reinforce the convictions of Christians in this matter, he lists the absurd conclusions that must follow from its denial: Christ has not risen; his preaching and the faith of the people is in vain. Then he draws the final conclusion: "If Christ has not risen, vain is your faith, for you are still in your sins." (1 Cor 15,13–17) Admittedly, this phrase is open to several interpretations, yet it can be argued that any adequate interpretation must include the fact that Christ's resurrection is a direct cause of the remission of sins and of redemption. When Paul stresses that the faith of Christians would be vain without the resurrection, he does not mean that it will be lacking an object but would be ineffectual or unavailing. The sense is that without the resurrection, faith is valueless; consequently there is no forgiveness of sins. The resurrection, therefore, is significant not only as a motive of credibility but, more remarkably, as a direct cause of the forgiveness of sins.

One of the more celebrated and extensively debated texts relative to this question is Romans 4,25: "Jesus . . . who was delivered up for our sins and rose again for our justification." The Greek Fathers offered an uncomplicated interpretation of this verse by considering the death and resurrection of Christ as co-causes of the redemption. While they made no attempt to state the function of the resurrection as distinct from the death of Christ, their testimony is important because of their strong assertion that the purpose of the resurrection was the justification of man. The Latin Fathers recognized that Paul linked the death and resurrection of Christ, but also distinguished them. With this distinction prominent in their thinking, they tried to present Paul's thought as part of an integrated theology and to explain the distinct roles of the resurrection and death. This procedure led them to minimize the causality of the resurrection and to attribute to it an exclusively moral value; the resurrection was looked upon as a motive of faith or a guarantee of the effectiveness of Christ's death for redemption. The death of Christ was regarded as the exclusive cause of redemption while the resurrection was explained as an epilogue of the death and not a cause in any real sense.

St. Augustine

Not all the Latin Fathers relegated the resurrection to a secondary role in the redemption. In at least one of his sermons, St. Augustine presented Romans 4,25 as evidence of the causal connection between the resurrection and redemption. Going beyond the Greek Fathers, he distinguished between the death and resurrection with regard to the precise effect each one of them produced: "Just as we are brought into being by his death, so by his resurrection we come to maturity." This statement was then clarified: "Let us be freed from sin by his cross; let us therefore lay down what evil we have committed so that we may be able to be justified by his resurrection. Indeed, you ought to emphasize the distinction between 'He was delivered up for our sins' and 'He rose again for our justification'. . . . Let sin die, then, and let justice rise again." (*Sermon* 236)

The significance of this interpretation lies in the fact that Augustine did not study the redemption in an exclusively legal framework. Christ's work is not simply a matter of making retribution to God but also of dissolving the estrangement between God and man and returning man to the supernatural life of justice. The resurrection fits into the plan and the work of redemption as the cause of this new life of justice. Augustine was not consistent in this interpretation of Romans 4,25, but these views just discussed had some impact on later theologians.

St. Thomas

Further clarification of the distinct roles of the death and resurrection of Christ is provided by St. Thomas. In his comments on Romans 4,25, he points out that the resurrection of Christ, unlike his death, cannot be said to have earned the redemption; since Christ was dead and therefore beyond merit his resurrection could not be a meritorious cause of redemption. From this fact he concludes that in addition to the meritorious value of Christ's death it must be recognized that both the death and resurrection caused redemption by way of efficient causality. This "efficiency" spoken of by St. Thomas involves the direct production of the effect by God who uses these mysteries as instruments for this purpose. (Cf. p. 24.) God uses these mysteries in keeping with the nature of each of them and the particular effect he works through them corresponds in some way to the nature of the death and resurrection. He concludes that the death of Christ is the cause of the removal of sins, "while the resurrection by which he returns to the life of glory is the cause of our justification through which we return to the newness of justice." (*On Romans,* 4,3)

St. Thomas' interpretation of Romans 4,25 is noteworthy for several reasons: his expansion of the basis of redemption beyond its legal aspects; his forthright assignment of a proper causality to the resurrection; and his presentation of the redemptive values of the death and resurrection in the framework of the scholastic explanation of causality. He pursues these same points in other parts of his commentary on Romans. God, the principal agent of redemption, uses the human nature of Christ and the mysteries of this human nature as instruments to bring the redemption to completion. Since they are instruments, the mysteries of Christ's life, death and resurrection exert a direct causality on the effect. These mysteries differ from one another, hence the contribution that each makes to the total effect will be different. The particular effect of each mystery will be exemplified by the character of the mystery. Thus, through the death of Christ we die to sin and through his resurrection we live unto God. (*On Romans,* 6,2)

In the *Summa Theologiae,* this view of redemption is spelled out in more detail. In discussing the causality of the death of Christ, St. Thomas distinguishes between the act of dying and the state of death. To the former he attributes the legal or juridic effects of the redemption such as merit; to the latter he refers efficient causality. Even in death, the humanity of Christ remains united to the divinity and is the instrument of the divinity. It can exercise direct, efficient causality to bring the redemption to perfection. (*S.Th.,* 3,50,6)

Meeting the objection that the passion of Christ was sufficient to accomplish the salvation of man, St. Thomas deals more explicitly with the function of the resurrection. He returns to the idea that each of the mysteries of Christ produce an effect that is proper to it, and argues that the passion of Christ removed the evil of sin, while the resurrection had the dual effect of providing man with the supernatural goods of justification and enabling him to begin to enjoy them. (*S.Th.*, 3,53,1 and ad 3)

In his concern to clarify the causality of the resurrection, St. Thomas distinguishes between its *efficient* and *exemplary* causality. With regard to the latter, he remarks that the resurrection of souls from sin is patterned after the model of Christ's bodily resurrection from the dead; for this reason, we should try to conform ourselves to him in every respect. In dealing with efficient causality, he states flatly that the resurrection is an instrument of the divinity and as such it is an efficient cause of the resurrection of souls from sin. This is to say that it contributes directly to the communication of supernatural life which replaces death of sin. (*S.Th.*, 3,56,2)

Answering again the objection raised concerning the superfluity of the resurrection in view of the values of the passion, he argues that the passion and resurrection are used by the divinity as instruments to effect the total justification of man. If Christ's death, then, is to be understood as the exemplary cause of our death to sin and the resurrection the exemplary cause of the new life of grace, it may be concluded that the death is the efficient cause of the remission of sin and the resurrection the efficient cause of the communication of grace. (*S.Th.*, 3,56,2 ad 4)

This discussion of St. Thomas' presentation of the redemptive value of the resurrection has been aimed at establishing an interpretation of the mind of St. Paul and showing the development of theological tradition on the causality of the resurrection. The conclusion of the discussion is that the redemptive acts of Christ most definitely include his resurrection from the dead. The data of revelation explained by theological tradition present the resurrection in terms that do not allow it to be relegated to a relatively minor function in the work of redemption. Together with the death of Christ, in a different but no less real way, it is a cause of redemption.

Some Possible Objections

It may be objected that this insistence on considering the resurrection as a co-cause of the redemption will dilute the legal or juridic elements of the redemption to the point of insignificance. It can be urged that the legal view of the redemption is found in the New Testament, has been asserted by the Church, and is prominent in theological tradition. Nor can there be any doubt about the validity of the legal aspects of the redemptive work of Christ. An extended discussion of the meritorious, satisfactory, and liberative effects of Christ's redemptive work is reserved for Chapter 5. The complaint that is implicit in this discussion of the causality of the resurrection has to do with presentation of the redemption as an exclusively legal matter. The hope that is implicit in this insistence on the importance of the resurrection is that a more complete and more balanced picture of the redemption will emerge.

The theologian's task is to present and explain the data of revelation. To minimize the function of the resurrection in the work of redemption is to neglect a very considerable and vital part of the revealed data. The theologian must take all the data as they are presented and work to achieve an integrated view of the whole. Emphasis is placed on the resurrection with an eye to this work of integration.

It may, on the other hand, be argued that the relegation of the resurrection to a minor and indirect function in the redemption will logically lead to the view that the redemption is a legal fiction in which the work of Christ is imputed to the sinner without his being changed interiorly. (D821) The reason for making this rather extreme charge is that if the resurrection is withdrawn as a direct cause of redemption there is no real explanation of the communication of grace which changes man interiorly. Since the positive sanctification of man is attributed to the resurrection, the causality of the resurrection must be exerted if this vital aspect of the redemption is to be verified.

Another possible source of objection is the great emphasis placed by the Church on the death of Christ. The impression can be given that the death of Christ, exclusive of any other mystery, is the decisive act of the redemption. A typical example of this emphasis is provided by Pius XII: "That he completed his work on the gibbet of the cross is the unanimous teaching of the holy Fathers . . . through his triumph on the cross . . . he won power and dominion over the gentiles . . . by his blood shed on the cross God's anger was averted and all the heavenly gifts . . . could then flow from the fountains of our savior for the salvation of men." (Encyclical *Mystici Corporis,* "On the Mystical Body," *AAS* 35 [1943], 205f) Superficially, this passage seems to leave no room for the resurrection as a cause of the redemption.

This problem is best resolved by examining it in context. In the Epistle to the Romans, St. Paul attributes justification to Christ's death (Rom 5,9), and in another connection to his resurrection. (Rom 4,25) St. Thomas speaks of justification as involving death to sin and the achievement of supernatural life; the first is the proper effect of the death of Christ, the second the effect of the resurrection. But it must be remembered that in justification there are not physically distinguishable stages of death and new life. Justification is a single reality. Man is justified in the simplicity of a single act of God and the human nature of Christ. In the achievement of this single effect, the death and resurrection of Christ are two causes but so linked with one another that they produce the one effect of redemption with a single causality. It may be said that the life, death, resurrection, and ascension of Christ constitute one redemptive act producing the total effect.

Given this context, it can be seen that attributing redemption to any one of the causes is legitimate since any one of them implies the others and cannot be properly explained in independence of the others. Moreover, it is legitimate to distinguish the formalities (remission of sins by the infusion of grace) within the single total effect, and to speak of these as the particular effects of those mysteries which exemplify them. (*S.Th.*, 3, 53, 1 ad 3; 56,1 ad 4)

THE ASCENSION OF CHRIST

The saving purpose of Christ's ascension is sung out by the Church in the Preface for the Feast of the Ascension: "who . . . was lifted up into heaven, so that he might make us partakers of his godhead." Accepting the fact that the ascension has contributed to the redemption and is therefore a cause of it, the theologian has the task of establishing the precise function of this mystery in the plan and work of redemption.

The ascension must be studied in close relationship to the resurrection. This is the climax of Christ's glorification. St. Peter speaks of it as an enthronement of Christ risen from the dead: "Therefore, let all the house of Israel know most assuredly that God has made both Lord and Christ, this Jesus whom you crucified." (Ac 2,36) But the ascension is not simply a personal glorification and vindication of Christ by the Father, it has implications for all men. Christ leaves the world and goes to the Father (Jn 16,28); there he is seated at the right hand of the Father (Col 3,1), and being thus established with the Father and constituted the Lord of all, he can send the Holy Spirit. (Jn 14,16) The ascension is the climax of Christ's earthly mission when he becomes in the full sense "the cause of eternal salvation." (Heb 5,9)

St. Thomas's discussion of the ascension as a cause of salvation depends on biblical themes. (*S.Th.*, 3,57,6) Citing St. John, "I go and prepare a place for you" (Jn 14,2), he points out that Christ as the head of his body will be followed by his members. Thus, Christ's ascension is effective for our salvation since the return to the Father has already been inaugurated by Christ, the head, to whom we are united. The entrance of Christ into heaven is compared to the entrance of the high priest into the sanctuary of the temple to serve God on behalf of the people. Filling out this image, Thomas speaks of Christ's presence as making him competent "to save those who come to God through him, since he lives always to make intercession for them." (Heb 7,25) Finally, the ascension has established Jesus in heaven as Lord and Christ, able to distribute divine gifts to men. "He who descended, he it is who ascended also above all the heavens, that he might fill all things." (Eph 4,10)

Like the resurrection, the ascension is an instrument used by the divinity to bring the redemption to completion. Christ did not merit by ascending into heaven; there is no merit after death. But this mystery was used by the divinity as an efficient instrumental cause of redemption and becomes operative as the direct cause of the ascension of men into heaven. (*S.Th.*, 3,57,6 ad 1 and ad 2)

Conclusion

This attempt to identify the decisive acts of the redemption leads to the conclusion that all the activity of Christ on earth, before and after his death, constitutes a single cause of redemption. At this point, it is possible to see each and all of these mysteries as instruments used by God to bring about the rescue of man from sin. It is evident that it is the Father who reconciles us to himself in Christ. (2 Cor 5,18)

When the decisive character of the complexus of mysteries from conception to ascension is recognized, the richness of the divine plan can be appreciated. Joining humanity and divinity in his own person and being made one with every human being, Christ has done all things necessary to dissolve the enmity between God and man. He has met the requirements of justice, earned the supernatural life for men, and become a "life-giving spirit" (1 Cor 15,45), capable of joining all men to himself and in himself to the Father.

CHAPTER FOUR

THE SACRIFICE OF CHRIST

When the redemptive acts of Christ have been identified and their function as instruments of the divinity has been determined, the theologian must turn his attention to a deeper analysis of these acts. It is not enough to say that God used these acts to effect the redemption. Their proper character and meaning must be explained. Nor can the theologian be satisfied with the fact that these acts were performed by a sinless agent, infinite in dignity and uniquely one with all men. While this aspect of Christ's activity is significant, it does not provide an insight into the nature of these acts as they were performed by him. Christ is the new and eternal high priest and as such he "is appointed for men in the things that pertain to God, that he may offer gifts and sacrifices for sins." (Heb 5,1) The priesthood of Christ is basic to his potential for saving all men; and this potential is realized in the offering of sacrifice. This chapter is concerned with the critically redemptive acts of Christ as constituting a sacrifice. This fact lies at the core of the redemptive activity of Christ.

The name "sacrifice" can be given to any act which is demonstrative of the religious spirit of man. In this sense a good act, done for God and expressive of man's submission to God, can be called a sacrifice. (*S.Th.*, 3,22,2) All the activity of Christ was sacrificial in this sense. There was no act of Christ that was not good and pleasing to the Father, no act that was not God-centered and practically submissive to the divine primacy. The concern of these pages will be to establish the fact that Christ offered sacrifice in a more restricted sense, and that this sacrificial action is found in his death and resurrection.

PRIESTHOOD AND SACRIFICE

That Christ offered a sacrifice is to be expected from the fact that he was constituted a priest by the incarnation. The very definition of priest includes the ability to offer sacrifice. (Heb 5,1) The link between priest and sacrifice is reflected in the teaching of the Church. The anathemas of St. Cyril include this statement: "Christ was made a high priest and apostle of our praise and in the odor of fragrance offered himself to God and the Father for us." (D122) The Council of Trent, concerned specifically with the sacrificial nature of the Mass and laying the foundations of this doctrine, speaks of Christ as "another priest according to the order of Melchisedech." His work as priest is first described generally in terms of leading men to perfection, and then stated more exactly: "Though he was about to offer himself once to God the Father upon the altar of the cross by the mediation of death, that he might accomplish an eternal redemption. . . ." (D938) On the Feast of Christ the King, the Church sings these words: "Father, who with the oil of gladness hast anointed thine only-begotten Son, our Lord Jesus Christ, as eternal high priest and universal king, that offering himself on the altar of the cross as an immaculate host and peace offering, he might complete the mysteries of human redemption." (Preface)

The offering of sacrifice is part of the task of mediation to which the priest is deputed. He acts as a public officer in the discharge of this task, representing all the people and acting in the name of the whole society. (*S.Th.*, $2^{a}2^{ae}$,86,2) Christ's eligibility for the offering of sacrifice is evident from his position as mediator and priest as a result of the incarnation. His place at the head of the human race illumines the depth and scope of his priestly office. He does not act in the name of a particular society of a certain place and time, but in the name of all men of all places and times. His solidarity with all men, the fact that he is in a real sense a summary or recapitulation of all, enhances his ability to represent them as a public officer of religion.

ANALYSIS OF SACRIFICE

Sacrifice, as a special act of religious cult, is an act or complexus of acts which give praise to God, express reverence for him, and manifest man's sense of absolute dependence on him. (*S.Th.*, $2^{a}2^{ae}$,85,3) In its outward expression it is usually defined as the offering of a sensible object, accompanied by some change in the object, legitimately made to God alone by a competent minister to acknowledge God's supreme dominion and, in the case of fallen nature, to make reparation to God for sin. Sacrifice can be described as a rite in which man gives something to God as an earnest of his internal dedication of himself to God. When man offers a tangible gift to God, this action is designed to be an external expression of man's interior sentiments.

Sacrifice originates in man's knowledge of God's dominion over him, is animated by his inner spirit of subjection to God, and can be verified formally (ritually) in the external, perceptible proffering of a gift to God. (*S.Th.*, $2^{a}2^{ae}$,85,2) The offering of a sacrifice to anyone less than God would be idolatrous. (*S.Th.*, $2^{a}2^{ae}$,85,2)

Sacrifice is not a private venture but a public act which is executed in the name of society. There is nothing out of order in an individual's expressing his spirit in a sacrificial rite of his own design and by his own initiative. (*S.Th.*, 3,85,1) But when authority intervenes, the sacrifice becomes a public act and must be offered by one who is officially delegated for this purpose. This is the priest who performs the rite as the agent of the community and in virtue of being deputed by authority. (*S.Th.*, $2^{a}2^{ae}$,85,4) When the redemptive sacrifice of Christ is being discussed, it is obvious enough that an act of public worship is involved. The determination of the rite by the Father is part of his plan to save all men; the designation and consecration of Christ as the priest of the sacrifice and the agent of the entire human community is an effect of the incarnation.

Since sacrifice is prompted and animated by man's inner sentiments toward God, it will be expressive of his regret for sin. Sin has affected man's relationship with God and must be taken into account when he turns to God. Sacrifice is a public acknowledgment of God's supremacy and at the same time a public testimony to man's sorrow for sin, a petition to God for pardon, and an act of satisfaction.

Unity of Sacrificial Action

Sacrificial action in the ancient world, including Israel, was normally made up of three elements, the offering of an object (the victim), its immolation, and a sacred meal in which the food that is now the deity's possession is eaten by the worshipper. The rite involves distinct actions which fit together to form one and the same act of sacrifice. In it the victim is first given to God (or a god), who then returns it charged with a divine or numinous quality. The actual immolation of the victim derives its meaning only from the offering, and the offering in turn must be consummated in some sign of union or communion. Christ did not actually slay himself but permitted others to do it; his function as priest was to offer this slaying, and thus to render it sacrificial. (*S.Th*, 3,48,3 ad 3)

Value of Sacrifice

The worth of any sacrifice is found in its inner spirit, that is, in the genuineness of the interior dispositions which prompt the external offering. By its nature sacrifice is the sign of a spirit that is profoundly submissive to God. The value of a sacrifice before God is contingent upon the actual correspondence of man's spirit to this sign. This can be shown in the sacrifices of Cain and Abel. (Gn 4) Cain offered the fruits of the field and Abel the best of his flocks. Both offerings, it seems, should have been acceptable to God, but God looked with favor on Abel's sacrifice and rejected Cain's. The traditional rationale is that Cain's offering was not a true reflection of his spirit—the sign of complete submission did not correspond to the reality in Cain. (Gn 4,7) Abraham's sacrifice also illustrates this truth. God commanded Abraham to offer his son Isaac in sacrifice. Abraham's submission was complete and unhesitating; he followed God's directions and was on the point of destroying his son as the victim of a sacrifice. God stayed his hand, provided a substitute victim, and declared his pleasure with what Abraham had done. (Gn 22,1–18)

The fact that the value of sacrifice is derived from its inner spirit is very significant in understanding and evaluating the sacrifice of Christ. The worth of Christ's sacrificial action and its acceptability to God will depend not on the bitterness of his suffering and death but on the obedience and charity expressed by the suffering and death. Since there is no flaw in his dispositions and they correspond perfectly to the external dimensions of his sacrifice, his offering is acceptable to God and the effects of his sacrifice are realized.

Figures of Christ's Sacrifice

Christ's sacrifice can only be understood in terms of the sacrifices of the Old Testament which it fulfilled. Frequently the New Testament writers will describe Christ's sacrifice in terms that are intelligible only when read with some knowledge of these previous sacrifices. A brief study of the particular purposes and rites of these sacrifices is undertaken here to help in the theological penetration of Christ's sacrifice.

PASCHAL LAMB Christ is often described in the New Testament as the Paschal Lamb. St. Paul urged the Corinthians to purge themselves of all uncleanness with the approach of Easter, "for Christ, our passover, is sacrificed." (1 Cor 5,7; 1 Pt 1,19; Preface of Paschaltide) The reference is to the rite in which the Israelites sacrificed a lamb, sprinkled their doorposts with its blood, and, being thus identified as Israelites, were saved from the slaying of the firstborn, a punishment inflicted by God upon the Egyptians. (Ex 12) This sacrifice and its aftermath led to the escape of the Israelites from slavery to the Egyptians. (Ex 12,31ff) The sacrifice of the Paschal Lamb was an instrument of deliverance for Israel. The sacrifice of Christ was an instrument of deliverance for all men.

The circumstances of the sacrifice of the Paschal Lamb show forth the element of consecration, vital in the understanding of Christ's sacrifice. The sprinkling of the blood of the lamb had the effect of consecrating the Israelites in the sense that it separated them from the pagans and marked them off as God's people. Significantly, this separation of Israel from the Egyptians was a decisive factor in their liberation from slavery.

The sacrifice of Christ had the same function. St. John speaks of the sealing of "the servants of God on their foreheads" (Ap 7,3); the one hundred and forty-four thousand thus sealed are those who "have washed their robes and made them white in the blood of the Lamb." (Ap 7,14) These are the redeemed who stand before the throne of God free of all tribulation. "For the Lamb who is in the midst of the throne will shepherd them and guide them to the fountains of the waters of life, and God will wipe away every tear from their eyes." (Ap 7,15ff)

SACRIFICE OF THE COVENANT At the Last Supper, when Jesus said: "This cup is the new covenant in my blood which shall be shed for you" (Lk 22,20; 1 Cor 11,25; Mt 26,28; Mk 14,24), the witnesses were undoubtedly reminded of the sacrifice offered by Moses to seal the old covenant. (Ex 24) Moses had offered burnt sacrifices and peace offerings, poured out part of the blood of the victims at the foot of the altar, and sprinkled the people with the rest of the blood. While sprinkling them, he said: "this is the blood of the covenant which the Lord has made with you." (Ex 24,8) The sacrifice and the sprinkling of the blood on the people had the effect of consecrating Israel as God's own people and distinguishing them from all others.

This theme is given prominence in the New Testament with reference to the sacrifice of Christ. Christ is the mediator of a new covenant (Heb 9,15) and the shedding of his blood has been the instrument of the new agreement. (Heb 9,12) The sacrifice of himself to destroy sin has established a new people of God which has been purchased by the blood of Christ. (Ac 20,28; Ap 5,9) This new people of God is thus united to God by the blood of Christ.

SACRIFICE OF EXPIATION The theme of expiation is strong in the New Testament. Christ is said to have offered himself in a sacrifice of expiation or propitiation. St. Paul speaks of justice coming "through the redemption which is in Christ Jesus, whom God set forth as a propitiation by his blood." (Rom 3,25) This calls to mind the annual sacrifice of expiation on the solemn day of *Kippurim* and implies that the sacrifice of Christ was the perfect sacrifice for sin.

The mention of the blood of Christ as the instrument of propitiation recalls the prescription of the Law that the blood of the victim is to be sprinkled seven times toward the propitiatory or mercy seat. (Lv 16,14) The purpose of this sprinkling was to "expiate the sanctuary from the uncleanness of the children of Israel, and from their transgressions, and all their sins." (Lv 16,16) Again, as in the other sacrifices mentioned, the purpose to be achieved by this rite is consecration. Since the holy places had been polluted by the sins of the people, they needed purification before "the glory of God" (Ez 10,18ff) will return to them. This is to reconsecrate them to God.

The function of blood in this rite of purification and consecration is worth noting. This shedding-of-blood ritual has erroneously been interpreted as a punishment inflicted upon a substitute for sinful man. But, while this idea of chastisement might be seen in the immolation of the victim, the more important fact is that the Jews considered blood the basic stuff of life—"the life of the flesh is in the blood." (Lv 17,11) As the bearer of life and identified with life, blood would be considered a divine reality. When it is sprinkled on an object or person, it can purify and consecrate.

Analysis of Sacrifices of the Old Law

Recognizing the obvious differences between the figure in which an inanimate or at most an irrational victim is offered to God by an imperfect priesthood and the reality in which the incarnate Son of God offers himself in his human nature, there are nonetheless aspects of the sacrifices of the Old Law which provide insights into the dynamics of Christ's sacrifice. In the former sacrifices, the meaning of sacrifice is spelled out in explicit terms. This allows for the application of these details to the sacrifice of Christ and consequently a deeper penetration of it.

The first significant fact is that sacrifice includes the making of a gift to God. The purpose of the presentation is that a good should be received by God. God's approval of what man had done was not enough. What was looked for was that God should take hold of the gift so that it would be his possession and no longer man's. No sacrifice was considered complete until the gift or victim was actually accepted by God.

Several devices were used to bring about and signify this acceptance. The destruction of the victim was one, but this seems to have been merely preparatory. Another was the placing of the gift on an altar. This sacred stone was the table of God and represented God himself. The placing of gifts on the altar meant putting them in God's hands. The effect of these rites was to transfer the victim to the dominion of God. In this way, the victim became a consecrated or divine thing. The meaning of these rites was that to sacrifice an object was literally to "sanctify a victim." (Dt 15,19) As a result of the sacrifice it was filled with the holiness of God. This holiness flowed into anyone who touched the victim (Lv 6,20); whoever partook of the victim obviously entered into the closest communion with God.

The same notions of the acceptance of the victim by God (involving its consecration) and of communion with God by those who eat the sacred food are found in the New Testament. The altar is said to sanctify the victim that is placed on it and thereby transferred to God. (Mt 23,19) Those who eat the victim of a sacrifice are said to be partakers of the altar. When the altar is representative of God, this results in union with God; on the other hand, the sacrifices of the pagans involve association with the devils to whom they offer sacrifice. (1 Cor 10,18–21)

The purpose of sacrifice under both covenants is always union with God. This has already been mentioned in relation to God's acceptance of the gift, but is worthy of more explicit note. Ordinarily, man entered into a close relationship with God in the sacrificial meal. Having offered his gifts to God and transferred them to his dominion, man is then invited to sit down at God's table and to partake of the gifts. They have been given to God but are now returned to man after being sanctified through consecration to the divinity. Man becomes God's guest, eating the now sacred food at God's invitation and entering into a new intimacy with him. While this part of the ritual was sometimes foregone in view of Israel's developed sense of sin and fear of God, the sacrifices ordinarily included a sacrificial meal for the purposes of communion with God. It may be said that this is the normal movement of the sacrificial action.

The purpose of this analysis is to underline what God does in the sacrificial action. His acceptance of the victim, his sanctification of it, his communion with those who offer the victim and partake of it, are obviously essential to the complete action of sacrifice. Should the theologian restrict his study to the mechanics of the sacrificial action as they are performed by man and neglect these more ample considerations of the role of God, he would seriously stunt his investigation of Christ's sacrifice and its results. The cogency of these considerations will be apparent shortly when the function of Christ's resurrection in his sacrificial action is taken up.

THE SACRIFICE OF CALVARY

That Christ offered himself in sacrifice to his Father is prominent and central in the Church's teaching on the redemption. (D122, 938) In statements on the sacrifice of the Mass, the Council of Trent links the Mass with what Christ did on Calvary and explains the reality of the unbloody sacrifice in relation to Christ's action on Calvary: "This sacrifice [the Mass] was to re-present the bloody sacrifice which he accomplished on the cross once and for all." (D938) This point is pursued in greater detail: "In the divine sacrifice that is offered in the Mass, the same Christ who offered himself in a bloody manner on the altar of the cross is present and is offered in an unbloody manner . . . it is one and the same victim—he who now makes the offering through the ministry of priests and he who then offered himself on the cross." (D940; Encyclical *Mediator Dei*, "On the Sacred Liturgy," *AAS* 39 [1947], 547-52)

From these statements by the Church, the outline of Christ's sacrificial action can be seen. Christ is the priest of the sacrifice. Established in the priesthood by his Father at the incarnation, he was from that moment competent to offer sacrifice. In that direction he aimed his entire life. (Heb 10,1–10) As a priest, Christ was the agent of the entire human community of all times and places; he offered this sacrifice in the name of all men and on their behalf. Since Christ's sacrifice was an act of public worship, its form was determined by the decree and command of the Father. What Christ did was done freely, but the pattern of his action had been established by the Father.

Christ was also the victim offered as a gift to the Father. Previous sacrifices had always involved the donation to God of one of man's material possessions; in this case, the gift is not one of man's possessions but the divine-human priest himself. Like all sacrifices, Christ's was expressive of an inner spirit. He offered himself to the Father to manifest adoration and thanksgiving, to present propitiation and petition to the Father. The gift was directed to the Father, but by the very nature of the sacrifice, Christ could look forward to its effects in himself and in all other men. They would be his own glorification and perfect union with the Father, and the reunion of all men with the Father through him.

All these dimensions of Christ's sacrifice are apparent in the teaching of St. Paul. "Christ loved us and delivered himself up for us an offering and sacrifice to God to ascend in fragrant odor." (Eph 5,2) This statement is characteristic of Paul's description of the redemption. Christ loved the Church and delivered himself up for it, to sanctify it. (Gal 1,4) As the one mediator between God and man, he gave himself as a redemption for all. (1 Tim 2,6) Christ is our saviour "who gave himself for us that he might redeem us from all iniquity and cleanse for himself an acceptable people." (Ti 2,13f)

Texts such as these indicate the fact, and something of the nature, of Christ's sacrifice. To say that Christ gave himself is to say that Christ the priest offered himself as victim to the Father. His act of offering is expressed in the exclamation "Father, into your hands I commend my spirit." (Lk 23,46) These words are a summary statement of the theme of his whole life, which was sacrificial. From the moment of his conception all that he thought, did, said, and suffered was aimed at this free giving of himself. (Heb 10,5–10; Mt 20,28) The circumstances of his arrest, trial, and execution show the voluntary nature of his surrender to his enemies and imply that this surrender is a giving of himself in the sense that he is positively offering himself. (Cf. above, pp. 41-42; Jn 10, 17f; *S.Th.*, 3,47,1.) The surrender of Christ to his executioners and to the destructive work they would do is the priestly act of offering himself to the Father by way of the sign of destruction.

Like other sacrifices, the value of Christ's offering of himself must be measured first by the perfection of his inner dispositions. Christ's sacrificial action was anything but a formalized gesture of submission to God. Christ is sinless. His holiness is unique and unflawed; there can be no fault found with his habitual dispositions and no suspicion that there is a discrepancy between his inner spirit and the nature of his sacrificial action. The perfection of Christ's inner spirit can be gauged from his obedience and love. (Phil 2,8; 1 Jn 3,16) These animate his activity in the sense that they make it God-centered and give it value before God. They are also the "soul" of his sacrificial activity, reflected perfectly in the external aspects of the sacrifice.

The unique value of Christ's sacrifice can be known from the value of the victim. In other sacrifices, the value of the offering may have been great, but it was always limited. When Christ offered himself, the value of the victim was charged with infinity. (Heb 9,13f) The dignity and holiness of the priest and the worth of the victim make the sacrifice of Christ far superior to any other that had been or could have been offered.

The superiority of Christ's sacrifice is prominently featured in the Epistle to the Hebrews. Christ's priestly holiness (Heb 7,26) and his infinite worth as a victim (Heb 9,14) are the basis for the transcendence of his sacrifice. In view of this fact, the effectiveness of Christ's sacrifice for the sanctification of all men is spelled out. By means of his sacrifice, Christ achieved "an eternal redemption." (Heb 9,12) His blood offered to God cleansed our "conscience from dead works to serve the living God." (Heb 9,14) Although the levitical priesthood had offered many ineffective sacrifices, "Christ was offered once to take away the sins of many." (Heb 9,28) To discuss the effectiveness of Christ's sacrifice for the redemption of all men, it is necessary to return to his resurrection and to determine its function in the full sacrificial action.

CHRIST'S SACRIFICE AND THE RESURRECTION

Death upon the cross has often been looked upon as the consummation of Christ's sacrifice. This, of course, is quite erroneous. Studied in terms of what man does, the sacrifice of Christ achieved a *completion* with the destruction of the victim; if the resurrection is thought to be mere epilogue to the essential activity of Christ on the cross, however, the outlines of this sacrifice will be distorted and the explanation of its effectiveness will be incomplete. Two elements of sacrifice are especially cogent to the theologian who seeks the rightful place of the resurrection in the sacrifice of Christ. The first is the undeniable fact that God takes part in the sacrificial action by taking possession of the victim and in some way consecrating and sanctifying it. The second is the fact that the sacrificial action is designed to bring about the union of God and man. The purpose of this discussion is to demonstrate that these essential aspects of the sacrificial action are found in the resurrection of Christ. The redemption of man by Christ's sacrifice is the *paschal* mystery. (Preface of Paschaltide) The resurrection must be recognized as an essential part of the sacrifice.

Acceptance of Christ's Sacrifice

If sacrifice is the offering of a gift to God in such a way that God takes full possession of it, a question about the sacrifice of Christ comes to mind. How can it be said that the Father did not have complete possession of Christ before the resurrection? The God-man was one with the Father in the unity of the divine essence. At the same time, his human nature was immersed deep in the divinity because of the union of natures. In reply to the difficulty, it can be pointed out that his human existence did not share to the utmost of its potential in the glory of the divinity before the resurrection. Despite Christ's possession of the beatific vision, his human nature was adapted in its entirety to the world in need of salvation. It was therefore capable of being taken over more completely by the divinity and in that sense eligible to be given to the Father.

When Christ said "I sanctify myself" (Jn 17,19), he meant that he was making this gift of himself to the Father, consecrating himself to the Father that the Father might take more perfect possession of him and thereby render him sacred or holy. A creature is sanctified by leaving the profane world as far as this is possible and dedicating himself to God or penetrating the sphere of the divine being. This involves separation from the profane world by self-oblation and passage into the possession of God. In the case of Christ, this was accomplished by the complete glorification of his human nature. Christ prayed: "Father, glorify your Son." (Jn 17,1) He was asking that the Father might take complete possession of him and thus set him apart as one holy and consecrated, accepted by God as a gift. The glorification of Christ is the Father's acceptance of the sacrifice, the final receiving of Christ the victim and gift, his ultimate sanctification. This divine activity belongs to the sacrificial action. The sacrifice of Christ is simply not complete without it.

The Epistle to the Hebrews sketches out the function of the resurrection as the completion of the redemptive sacrifice in terms of the sacrifice of atonement offered annually by the Jews. In this sacrifice, the priest immolated a bull and a goat outside the sanctuary, took their blood into the Holy of Holies which was the dwelling place of God, and sprinkled the blood on the Ark. In this, the victim was given over as far as possible into the possession of God. When Christ offered sacrifice, he offered himself outside the sanctuary of heaven, that is on earth; this was his passion and death on Calvary. As in the sacrifice of atonement, Christ the victim was immolated only to be brought more perfectly into God's possession. His immolation was but a preparation. He entered into the reserved sanctuary of the divinity by being raised up in glory. (Heb 9,11–12) By glorifying Christ the Father took complete possession of him, and in this way signified his acceptance of the sacrifice.

Another aspect of the sacrificial action is described in the Epistle to the Hebrews: the offering of the victim was consummated by the victim's being drawn into the divine perfection, the one offering the sacrifice gaining access to God and thereby attaining perfection. The offering and destruction had the effect of removing sin. This process was brought to completion by the one who offered the sacrifice. Through his personal access to God he received a certain perfection from God. The sacrifices of the Old Law, however, never achieved their purpose of bringing those who offered them to perfection. (Heb 10,1) The reason was that the victim did not achieve its own perfection by being drawn into the divine perfection. The imperfections of these sacrifices caused them to fall short of this goal. They did not have their conclusion in God.

The sacrifice of Christ, on the other hand, was not limited by imperfections; it achieved its consummation in God. The glorification of Christ was the conclusion of his sacrifice. It involved his being drawn into the divine perfection. Christ's sacrifice removed sin because the process of sacrifice was unimpeded and culminated in his glorification, placing him at the right hand of God. (Heb 10,11–14)

Studied from this vantage point, sacrifice can be seen to be a movement of man to God. Only in the sacrifice of Christ is this movement brought to completion because his resurrection brought him to perfection, completely in the possession of his Father. Without the resurrection, the sacrificial action would have been mutilated, incomplete, and ineffective for redemption.

Communion and Sacrifice

Sacrifice is the making of a gift to God by man. It is designed to form a bond between man and God, to establish an intimate relation between them. In the sacrifices of the Old Law, intimacy between God and man was achieved through the sacrificial meal. Having placed his gifts on God's table, thereby transferring ownership of them to God, man entered into a communion with God by sharing in these gifts. God receives gifts from man that he may return them to him after they have been consecrated to the divinity and sanctified. The sacred meal was the normal conclusion of the sacrificial rite since in it the goal of communion with God was realized.

The New Testament writers emphasize the communion with God when they compare Christ's sacrifice to that of the Paschal Lamb. (1 Cor 5,7; 1 Pt 1,18f) The paschal sacrifice included a sacrificial banquet (Ex 12,8) through which union with God was achieved. This was a preview of Christ's sacrifice. The body of Christ was delivered up for his disciples. As part of the complete sacrificial action they take it and eat it in a rite which joins them to God. (Lk 22,14–20) This eucharistic banquet eaten on earth is but an earthly anticipation of the messianic banquet to take place at the end of time. The messianic feast will be the inauguration of the kingdom and a prolongation of the eucharist. Christ himself will share this sacrificial meal with his disciples. (Mt 26,29)

The beginning of this celebration and the union with God that comes with it was in the resurrection of Christ. Christ glorified then entered the kingdom of his Father. He may be said to have sat down to the messianic banquet at that time. For Christ this was not the eating of a ritual meal with the Father but the immediate sharing in the divine life to a new degree of perfection. Given the union of his followers with Christ, they can be said to have already begun to take part in the messianic banquet in him. Later, united with Christ in glory and sharing with him in the divine life, they will achieve complete union with God when they actually join him in the eating of the great messianic banquet.

CONCLUSION

The sacrifice of Christ, like every true sacrifice, looks first to God. Originating in man's religious spirit, the movement of man signified by his gift is toward God. Passing through the stages of offering and immolation, man dedicates himself and his gift to God. God then takes possession of the gift, renders it holy, and unites man to himself.

Christ offered himself as a gift to God, was immolated on the cross and taken possession of by the Father in the resurrection. The union between Christ and all men points to the fact that he is not the only beneficiary of this sacrifice. The offering and the destruction were performed in the name of all men. The consecration and sanctification of Christ accomplished in the resurrection also affects all men. They are in Christ in some measure; when these changes in his condition took place they were potentially sanctified and glorified. When their relationship with Christ is brought to a further stage of perfection and they achieve actual membership in his mystical body through faith and baptism, their potential for sanctification will be realized. They will then begin to live in Christ, and be joined to the Father through Christ. The achievement of the beatific vision is still another realization of their potential for holiness and glory. The ultimate stage of perfection is attained with their bodily resurrection in Christ, when they will join him at the Father's table in the kingdom.

CHAPTER FIVE

THE EFFECTS OF CHRIST'S SACRIFICE

Once the sacrificial nature of Christ's redemptive activity has been recognized, the theologian should turn to the specific effects produced by this sacrifice. In view of the discussion in Chapter 4, it is apparent that Christ's sacrifice was accepted by God and was therefore successful in achieving the redemption of all men; but this was only an outline of the successful results of the sacrifice. More precise determination of these results is called for. The basis for this determination is found in the data of revelation.

Christ is the New Adam. His activity is designed to counteract the sin of the first Adam. The effects of his sacrifice can be expected to offset the effects of Adam's sin. If sin has resulted in the loss of gifts by man, Christ's sacrifice regains them for him. If sin has brought man into captivity, Christ's sacrifice liberates him. If sin has caused an enmity between God and man, Christ's sacrifice brings about a reconciliation. (Cf. above, pp. 6-11.) If sin has deprived God of glory, Christ's sacrifice is satisfactory in rendering to God superabundant glory. Seeing the work of Christ in this perspective, the theologian comes to examine it as a work of *merit,* of *liberation,* of *reconciliation,* and of *satisfaction.*

Since all of Christ's acts were an execution of the saving plan of the Father, which included the notion of a covenantal relation with a people made holy by election, these acts are performed in fulfillment of the terms of that agreement. A specific reward is promised by the Father to his covenanted people. His Son, in whom the life of that people is summed up, merits the reward of glory in the promised land of risen life after his passage through the desert of suffering and death.

CHRIST'S WORK OF MERIT

The Church has often spoken of the redemptive activity of Christ in terms of its meritorious value. To merit is to act freely, under the impulse of grace, in circumstances where God has promised a reward. If there is an equality between the act and the reward, the act is said to be *condignly* meritorious; if the only relation is one of equity, the act is said to be *congruously* meritorious. The shedding of Christ's blood "gained a great treasure for the Church militant." (D550) No one is ever freed from the domination of the devil "except through the merit of the mediator between God and men, our Lord Jesus Christ." (D711) The only remedy for original sin is the merit of Jesus Christ, and this merit is applied to men through the sacrament of baptism. (D790) Christ is the meritorious cause of our salvation. (D799) These samples of the Church's teaching show a consciousness of an "earning power" in the acts of Christ—a correspondence between deed and result—especially in his passion and death. This power looks to the acquisition of supernatural benefits for all men. This is not to say that these goods were immediately put into the possession of all men; having been acquired through the activity of Christ, they were made available for distribution.

In the New Testament Christ's work is not referred to explicitly as meritorious, but many statements descriptive of it cannot be understood except a certain earning power be attributed to it. St. Paul speaks of the origin of justification with the Father "who has blessed us with every spiritual blessing on high in Christ." (Eph 1,3) The full meaning of this statement includes the fact that man receives his supernatural gifts from the Father through Christ and by reason of his union with Christ, and also the fact that he receives them in view of what Christ has done for him. This is to say that supernatural benefits are available to man because of the earning power or the meritorious value of Christ's activity. The same kind of interpretation should be put on the statement that we have been brought to life with Christ, raised up with him and seated with him in heaven. (Eph 2,5f) This has been done by God "that he might show in the ages to come the overflowing riches of his grace in kindness towards us in Christ Jesus." (Eph 2,7)

It is universally held that only those acts of Christ performed before his death had meritorious value. (*S.Th.*, 3,19,3 ad 1) The period of merit began with the moment he was conceived, since from that time he had grace and an infused knowledge which enabled him to engage in thoroughgoing human activity. (*S.Th.*, 3,34,3) All the acts performed through his human nature from conception to death were meritorious and directed to the achievement of the redemption. The climax of this series of acts came in his passion and death; this was the consummation of all his meritorious activity and the act in which all else was contained and summarized. (*S.Th.*, 3,48,1 ad 3) It was crowned by his glorification—the instrumentality of the glorification of all mankind.

CHRIST'S REWARDS

The Church's faith is that Christ is the meritorious cause of our salvation (D799); that is to say, by his activity he recovered grace and the other gifts that had been forfeited for all men by Adam. In view of Christ's sacrificial spirit God returned grace to man even more abundantly than it had been possessed by Adam. He also gave to man the possibility of recovering through charity certain effects of the lost preternatural gifts of immortality and integrity.

A precise accounting of the rewards merited by Christ must start with what he merited for himself, for only thereby did he merit for his brothers. Christ earned the glorification of his body and the exaltation of his name. (Phil 2,8f; Jn 17,4f; Lk 24,26) In the concrete, this involved his resurrection, ascension, sitting at the right hand of the Father, and being given the power to judge the living and the dead. (*S.Th.*, 3,49,6) These mysteries of the glorious life of Christ were in direct consequence of the acts of his life, summed up in his passion and death as the obedient, suffering servant. His conformity to his Father's will produced in him a worthiness to be glorified in his human nature. In view of his holy deeds he was given glory by the Father as he had been promised. (Cf. p. 23.)

The glorification of Christ is essential to an understanding of the gifts he merited for all men, for it was his glorification earned by his passion and death which made him "a life-giving spirit." (1 Cor. 15,45) To fill out the picture of Christ as a life-giving spirit who has earned new life for all men, enabling them to proceed to the glory of the Father, it is necessary to recall that he is the new head of the human race. (Cf. pp. 27-32.) Not only is he the representative of all men and eligible to act in their name, he is mysteriously one with all men, and by reason of this solidarity with them he can be said to contain them within himself.

This solidarity is the basis for the conclusion that Christ's meritorious activity left a disposition or worthiness of reward in all men; the fact that they are *in Christ* and one with him leads to the recognition of their being disposed and rendered worthy by Christ's meritorious acts. Thus, in view of Christ's meritorious acts, all men, as members of his body, are benefited by the actions of Christ the head. (*S.Th.*, 3,19,4)

Christ's headship of the human race is based on the fact that he is the source of a new and supernatural life for all men. Christ began his human existence with the fullness of grace, the "grace of headship." The singular plenitude of his grace made him capable of communicating grace to every man. But this fullness of grace was held in check until the end of his life. When he had completed his meritorious acts and, as a result of these, taken his position as a life-giving spirit, the fullness of grace was released. In this fullness all men can share. The merits of Christ did not bring this supernatural life into existence for the first time. The treasure of grace won by Christ was actually in his possession from the beginning of his life. What he merited was the power to communicate it.

The study of Christ's merits in this context maintains perspective in the explanation of the causality of the redemption. Christ's merits are genuine causes of the redemption in the sense that they are instruments used by the divinity for this purpose. They lead to the glorification of Christ and, through the instrumentality of the mysteries of Christ's glorious life, they lead to the sanctification and glorification of man.

CHRIST'S WORK OF LIBERATION

Since the redemptive activity of the New Adam countered the various effects of sin in man, it is to be expected that it brought about the liberation of man from the slavery resulting from Adam's sin. This theme has been prominent in the teaching of the Church. It has been pointed out that Christ assumed a human nature to free man from the yoke of the devil. (D371) Similarly, that no human being was ever freed from the domination of the devil except through the merits of the one mediator between God and man (D711), and that Christ freed man from the effects of the sin of Adam, has also been indicated. (D536,790) The liberation of man from enslavement to the devil and sin is clearly presented as an effect of Christ's redemptive sacrifice.

It is significant that the Church speaks of the liberation of man from sin as having been accomplished by the payment of a price. Christ is said to have bought man back, ransomed, or redeemed him. The blood of Christ, sign of his death, is regarded as a price he freely paid to effect the release of men from sin, eternal punishment, and the powers of darkness. This idea appears in a phrase of the Bull *Unigenitus Dei Filius* of Pope Clement VI (A.D. 1343): "a drop of blood which . . . would have been sufficient for the redemption of the whole human race. . . ." (D550) The figure of buying back is found in the constant use of the word "redemption" to describe the saving work of Christ. (D794,993)

The teaching of the Church also indicates the condition of liberated man. Having been freed from the powers of darkness, the slavery of the Law, sin and eternal death, man is brought into the kingdom of God. (D938) He is adopted as a son of God (D794) and is reconciled to the Father unto eternal life. (D993) While this positive aspect of the work of liberation is not elaborated in the documents of the Church, it is presented clearly enough to be recognized as part of the full picture of the work of liberation. It becomes particularly cogent in integrating liberation with the other aspects of Christ's saving activity and in explaining the full effect of this activity.

The New Testament on Man's Liberation

The death of Christ under the figure of the payment of a price is prominent in the New Testament. One of the more outstanding testimonies to this aspect of his saving work is this statement: "the Son of Man has not come to be served but to serve, and to give his life as a ransom (*lýtron*) for many." (Mt 20,28; Mk 10,45) This passage echoes the fourth Servant Song (Is 53,11), where it is said that through his sufferings the servant shall justify many. The basic meaning of the substantive *lýtron* is a ransom paid for the release of a prisoner or guilty party (cf. Nm 35,31), a price given in exchange for deliverance. A cognate notion is that of the Old Testament *go'el* or bondsman, a role which Yahweh plays with respect to Israel. (Gn 48,16; Ex 6,6; Os 13,14) St. Paul expresses the ransom idea when he says: "You have been bought at a great price." (1 Cor 6,20) The inference to be drawn is that the people thus purchased do not belong to themselves but to God. (1 Cor 1,9; Ac 20,28) The First Epistle of St. Peter, too, is explicit about the payment of a price: "You know that you were redeemed from the vain manner of life handed down from your fathers, not with perishable things, with silver or gold, but with the precious blood of Christ. (1 Pt 1,18f)

The condition from which men were ransomed by Christ, described in 1 Peter as "the vain manner of life," has been sketched out in the discussion of sin and its effects. (Cf. pp. 5-11.) St. Paul describes this condition in many references to the effects of sin. He speaks of man under the yoke of sin of Adam, and of his liberation by the redeeming work of Christ. (Rom 3,9; 7,23; 6,18–22) Men are released from a slavery to the Law, spoken of by Paul as an effect of sin. (Rom 7,1–6) Men are liberated from slavery to the devil and in this is contained a liberation from death. (Col 1,13; 2,14f; 2 Tim 1,10) These ideas are re-echoed by St. John (Jn 12,31; 1 Jn 3,8) and again in the Epistle to the Hebrews. (Heb 2,14f)

Payment of the Ransom

The concept of the saving work of Christ as a liberation achieved through payment has been variously and, at times, badly misunderstood. Some of the Fathers, although presenting the *fact* of redemption soundly enough, spoke of Christ's paying the ransom of his blood to the devil. The influence of the devil in man's history and the description of man's salvation as an escape from the power of the devil into the kingdom of God (Jn 12,31) led them to think of Satan as having real rights over man and being the one competent to receive from the Lord the price of the ransom. These ideas were proposed by Origen, Gregory of Nyssa, and Ambrose; they have become known as the theory of "mythical redemption." This theory was generally rejected by the Fathers who found it repugnant that the blood of Christ should be offered to the enemy of the all-holy God.

Another line of reasoning saw man's escape from the domination of the devil as a result of his overextending himself in bringing about the death of Christ. Certain rights over man were permitted to the devil by God when man sinned. When the devil assaulted Christ who was without sin, he overstepped the boundaries set for him by God. The upshot was his loss of dominion over man and the liberation of man from his power. In illustrating this explanation, some of the Fathers (for example, Rufinus of Aquileia, *On the Creed,* 16) compared the devil to a fish who was attracted to the bait of Christ's human nature and snared by the hook of his divinity. This theory of the abuse of power does not concede to the devil any strict rights over man, but rather the usurpation of power through the use of deceit. (*S.Th.,* 3,48,4 ad 2) It does not call for the payment of any price to the devil, but rather the ransoming of man by the payment of a price to God. This line of reasoning was pursued by Hilary, Augustine, Leo the Great, and Thomas Aquinas.

The explanation involving the payment of a ransom to God and the consequent overthrow of the devil's dominion over man fits into the broader picture of the struggle between Christ and the devil prefigured in Genesis 3,15. This struggle, which resulted in the victory of Christ, has been a constant theme in the teaching of the Fathers and has become a prominent feature of the Church's references in the liturgy to the work of Christ. The hymn *Vexilla Regis Prodeunt* ("The Royal Banners Forward Flung") for Good Friday is an example. The theme is Christ's triumph. It begins with man's sin and his fall, through deceit, into Satan's power. God's plan set Christ in opposition to Satan. Christ was victorious over Satan by dying on the cross as a victim.

Sacrifice and the Payment of Ransom

Considerable light can be shed on Christ's ransoming of man when this aspect of his saving work is studied in the context of the paschal sacrifice. The propriety of this method is apparent from Paul's allusion to the liberation of the Israelites from the slavery of Egypt when he refers to the work of Christ as the buying back of man: "Jesus Christ . . . gave himself for us that he might redeem us from all iniquity and cleanse for himself an acceptable people, pursuing good works." (Ti 2,14) These words refer to the two great events in the history of Israel, the deliverance from Egypt and the making of the covenant of Sinai. This twofold intervention of God came to be regarded by the Jews as negative and positive aspects of the same reality: God frees his people from slavery that he may take them for his own and make them a holy people. (Ex 6,6f; Dt 7,6ff; Jer 31,32) This is a constant refrain in the history of salvation. God delivers his people from bondage and thereby acquires them for himself. This liberation and acquisition of the people is called a redemption. (Ps 129[130],7f)

The study of Christ's redemption of men is helpfully illumined by this context. It can be seen that the concern about the recipient of the price paid by Christ does not have much meaning. There can be no question of a specific price having been paid to the devil; since God is the redeemer, there can be no payment of a price made in any strict sense by God to himself. The release of man from the bondage of sin and the devil is verified; looking at this process against the background of the escape from Egypt, it is fittingly called a ransoming or redeeming of man. The shedding of Christ's blood and his death should be called a ransom (*lýtron*) because it was used by God to effect man's release from sin. But the payment of the price *to someone* does not enter into this divine deed. If one should insist on rounding out the figure of buying or ransoming it must be held that the ransom is paid to God, since Christ's blood was shed in sacrifice to him. But this consideration has no particular relevance in an understanding of the divine redemption of man. The negative aspect of his saving action–studied in connection with his redemption of Israel from Egypt–is quite complete without it. He is the sole actor on behalf of his people Israel in the one case, and in behalf of all mankind through his Son in the other.

The positive aspect of this process, or the "acquisition" of man by God, must be kept in view if we are to have a balanced picture of man's liberation by Christ. Man is acquired or purchased by God and thus becomes God's own. By coming into his possession he is consecrated to him and made holy. (1 Cor 6,20; 7,23) This underlines the fact that man's redemption by Christ–his liberation from bondage–terminates in the union of man with God. The basic force of the word "atonement" is also revealed–God has made man one with himself.

The function of sacrifice in Christ's liberation of man from sin is underlined when Christ's work of redemption is looked upon with reference to the freeing of Israel from slavery and the making of the covenant on Sinai. In each of these events the offering of sacrifice–terminating in a sacrificial meal–was the key action performed by man, having the effect of liberating the people and bringing them into God's possession. (Ex 12,43; 24,5) These effects of separation from the profane and sinful and consecration to God belong to the nature of sacrifice, both as an offering and, in its term, a communing.

The resurrection, too, is brought into focus as part of the sacrificial action and the inevitable complement of Christ's passion and death. It explains the positive part of the process of liberation, the acquisition of man by God. The acts of Christ on Calvary can be seen as effecting man's release from the bondage of sin; these acts are completed by the glorification of Christ, by which God acquires for himself and consecrates all men through Christ the head of the race. (*S.Th.*, 3,53,1 and ad 3; cf. pp. 65-69.)

CHRIST'S WORK OF SATISFACTION

Satisfaction is the recompense one makes to another for injury inflicted on him. The purpose of satisfaction is to meet the requirements of justice. In the case of man's fall it is God's justice, that is, his absolutely transcendent holiness, that has been derogated from. He alone knows how satisfaction is to be made. Two things are clear: any satisfaction will consist in external acknowledgment of his holiness; secondly, in no sense are the limited categories of human justice applicable here. Human sin gives rise to guilt, which involves the necessity of bearing the "wrath of God" (St. Thomas Aquinas, *On Truth,* 28,2), and of undergoing punishment for the offense. (*S.Th.,* $1^{a}2^{ae}$,87,1) In the Old Testament the burning anger (*charōn aph*) of the Lord is an analogous concept that describes his awesomeness, his essential character as uniquely numinous; it is not something to be confused with pique or passion in him, although all the language of the Bible is in that order. The act of satisfaction presents to God something that is at least as pleasing to him as the offense has been displeasing. (*S.Th.,* 3,48,2) The debt of punishment is resolved by the act of satisfaction which has a penal character, in that the guilty person freely inflicts a penalty on himself or willingly accepts a penalty inflicted by God. (*S.Th.,* $1^{a}2^{ae}$,87,6) Satisfaction thus viewed is a legal or juridic aspect of Christ's redemptive activity. The act of satisfaction in the redemptive acts of Christ is "recompense for personal injury" in the sense that it is directed to the restoration of the proper personal relationship between God and his sinful people.

This aspect of Christ's redemptive work was given particular prominence by St. Anselm in his *Why Did God Become Man?* (1,11–13) Although it had been part of the Church's teaching on the redemption from apostolic times, Anselm formulated the explanation in precise, legal terms. His work opened an area of doctrine that has been exploited by St. Thomas (*S.Th.,* 3,48,2) and most theologians since his time.

There have been many objections to the validity of the Anselmian explanation, based on the supposition that it presents the redemption as an exclusively legal transaction between God and man involving so much pain from Christ to make up for so much sin in man. Of course the boundaries of the redemption go far beyond any purely legal considerations. It cannot be denied, however, that the redemptive work of Christ is presented in the New Testament as a work of satisfaction (a juridical term). This idea the theologian must present as clearly as possible.

The Fact of Satisfaction

The most authoritative statements on the satisfactory value of Christ's redemptive acts were made by the Council of Trent. It is said that by his most holy passion on the wood of the cross Christ "made satisfaction for us to God the Father." (D799) Penitential acts are urged on all because then "we are made like to Christ Jesus who has satisfied for our sins." (D904) These statements are not definitions of this truth, but the very fact that they are *obiter dicta* is indicative that this doctrine is fundamental in the thinking of the Church on the redemption and is part of its ordinary teaching.

From these samples of magisterial statements two conclusions emerge. The first is the reality of the satisfactory value of Christ's redemptive activity. Without explaining the meaning of the word they are using, the Fathers of Trent stated flatly that Christ made *satisfaction* for us. They obviously intended this statement to be understood in the sense recognized by all theologians up to that period. The second conclusion is that Christ made satisfaction *for us*. This is the doctrine of vicarious satisfaction. It has been badly misunderstood and requires some explanation.

Vicarious Satisfaction

The fact that Christ has made satisfaction for all men has led some in the past to see him as a kind of universal sinner, burdened with the guilt of all and an odious figure in the eyes of his Father. They saw in the sufferings of Christ the vengeance of the Father who, regarding Christ with hatred for his burden of sin, inflicted on him a certain amount of pain which would compensate for the number and kind of sins he was guilty of before the Father. This would make the Father out a peevish tyrant, gratified by the suffering of man. In no way is this an acceptable description of God; nor can this analysis of Christ's redemptive work get around the basic repugnance of the notion that the guilt of personal fault is being transferred to an innocent party acting in behalf of the guilty one. There can be no transfer of guilt in any strict sense. (*S.Th.*, 1^a2^{ae},87,8; 2^a2^{ae},108,4)

The proper explanation of Christ's vicarious activity must begin with his oneness with all men. The new head of the human race can act in the name of all men and for their benefit. His unique solidarity with all men made him the official representative of the human race before God and made it possible for his work of satisfaction to have an effect in every man. Like members of a body, all men are affected by the activity of the head of the body. (*S.Th.*, 3,19,4; 48,2 ad 1) It must also be maintained that Christ remained free of all guilt, and that he was always loved by his Father. Christ assumed the responsibility of making satisfaction for the sins of men but not the guilt of their sins. He freely undertook to give to the Father something that was more pleasing than the sins of men had been hateful. He also took the responsibility of discharging the penalties due to men's sins. *This does not mean that Christ was punished in man's stead. He freely accepted, out of love and obedience, sufferings by which he freed men from the burden of suffering the penalty of eternal damnation.*

Christ's freedom from guilt and the fact that he was not punished for the sins of men has been called into question in view of several statements by St. Paul. The latter seems to speak of Christ as having been made a sinner by his Father: "For our sakes he made him to be sin who knew nothing of sin, so that in him we might become the justice of God." (2 Cor 5,21) The apparent difficulty is resolved if the expression "who knew nothing of sin" is taken as descriptive of Christ's moral condition and indicative of his guiltlessness. This leads to the conclusion that the expression "made him to be sin" cannot mean that Christ is identified with sin. The conclusion is reinforced by the fact that sin in this connection designates a power with which no one can be identified. The meaning of the verse is that Christ took on the condition (not the guilt) of sinful man. Having been made one with man, he assumed some of the liabilities of man under the power of sin. His reason was that in this condition he could gain benefits for all men with whom he had made himself to be one; men can take advantage of these benefits precisely because of their solidarity with Christ.

Another curious statement by St. Paul seems to attribute to Christ a state of condemnation: "Christ redeemed us from the curse of the Law, becoming a curse for us; for it is written, 'Cursed is everyone who hangs on a tree'." (Gal 3,13) Paul's reference is to the shameful circumstances of the death of Christ, condemned and executed as a blasphemer in the name of the divine Law. Christ is cursed, but not by his Father, nor by the Law, but only by men. Again, the reference indicates Christ's solidarity with sinful man by underlining the humiliations which afflict him as a result of it. These humiliations, the treason of his friends, abandonment by his disciples, condemnation by the religious chiefs of his nation, all enable him to demonstrate an incomparable love for sinful man, and by means of this love to effect the redemption.

The Acts of Satisfaction

The satisfactory works of Christ include all his human activity from his conception to his death. Still in the womb of his mother, Christ was capable of human acts which contributed to the satisfaction of justice. (Heb 10,5–10) Death ends the possibility of any man's making satisfaction, and this is presumed true of Christ. *The saving acts of Christ which followed his death contributed to the redemption, but not by way of satisfaction.*

The value of his acts of satisfaction can be measured from Christ's personal innocence, and from the fact that all his human acts were charged with obedience and charity. This interior spirit made all his deeds pleasing to his Father—at least as pleasing as the sins of men were displeasing; his acts were thus capable of offsetting the denial of God's glory implicit in man's sin. The "balance of justice" is not found in a certain degree of pain countering the offense given by a certain number of sins. The balance is found in the dignity and worth of the honor given to God countering the offense given by sin. (*S.Th.*, 3,48,2)

A more compelling consideration of the worth of Christ's satisfaction depends on the infinite dignity of the acts of the God-man. Each of them had infinite value because, although human acts, they were done by a divine person. Any one of them was more than sufficient to satisfy for man's sin. But in the design of God, all the individual acts were summarized in his passion and death; it is in this mystery that the completion and perfection of his satisfactory acts are found. When the lifetime of deeds and the singular value of his passion and death are taken into account, the superabundance of his satisfaction can be seen.

"Where the offense abounded, grace has abounded yet more." (Rom 5,20)

The Initiative of the Father

St. Paul provides a vital insight into the nature of the redemption and the place of satisfaction in the divine plan by indicating that the initiative for Christ's satisfactory works lies with the Father. Men are justified by the grace of God "through the redemption which is in Christ Jesus whom God has set forth as a propitiation by his blood, through faith, to manifest his justice." (Rom 3,24f) This statement puts the works of satisfaction performed by Christ into perspective as instruments of the divine purpose. The work of satisfaction, which obviously proceeds from the human nature of Christ, originates in the Father's love of all men. This human activity of its nature looks to the Father, yet it is a living instrumentality used by the Father to effect the redemption. It is important to maintain this perspective and to study all references to the propitiatory and satisfactory value of Christ's works in this context. (Cf. 1 Jn 2,2;4,10.)

This view of the satisfactory actions of Christ opens the way to recognition of the resurrection as part of the process by which the work of Christ was brought to perfection. There is no question of his making satisfaction by his resurrection and ascension; but the glorification of Christ by the Father complements his works of satisfaction. The acts of Christ up to and including his death satisfy the divine justice, and are used by the deity for that purpose. They also affect the human nature of Christ, making it an apt instrument to be used by the divinity as an efficient cause of the redemption, with particular reference to the *purification* of man (preparatory stage). The purification leads to the *reunion* of God and man; the divine instrument in this aspect of the redemption is the resurrection (perfective stage). (Cf. pp. 68-69.)

This explanation takes into consideration the fact that there is no real anger in God toward man and puts into context the analogous terms "pleasing" and "displeasing" with reference to God. God's love for man is uninterrupted; there can be no change in him. The satisfaction given to God by Christ is the Father's instrument for redeeming man. It should be seen as the means he uses to eliminate sin and open the way to man's reunion with God. The resurrection is used by God as the capstone or completion of acts of satisfaction, bringing all men once again into union with God in Christ and through Christ. The total picture of redemption, including the remission of sins and the communication of a new life, comes into focus when the resurrection is recognized as the complement of Christ's satisfactory work.

CHRIST'S WORK OF RECONCILIATION

The fact that the ultimate aim of Christ's work is the reconciliation of man to God has been part of the discussions of the last two chapters. This is the climactic effect of his redemptive activity. Christ's sacrifice with its meritorious, liberative, and satisfactory effects dissolves the enmity between God and man. With the end of the estrangement that is part of sin, man and God again enter the relation of mutual friendship that had characterized man's original condition. In this economy of redemption, the reunion of God and man takes place in Christ.

The Church is explicit in teaching this effect of the redemptive activity of Christ. In its decree on original sin, the Council of Trent stated: "He reconciled us to God in his blood, having become for us justice, sanctification, and redemption." (D790) Pope Paul IV, in an outline of the basic truths that must be held by faith, speaks of the submission of Christ to the cruel death on the cross "to redeem us from sins and from eternal death and to reunite us to the Father unto eternal life." (D993)

These statements of the Church reflect the teaching of St. Paul. In Paul's theology of redemption, emphasis is placed on the initiative of the Father in the work of reconciliation, and on the instrumentality of Christ and his activity. "For if when we were enemies we were reconciled to God by the death of his Son, much more, having been reconciled, shall we be saved by his life. And not this only, but we exult also in God through our Lord Jesus Christ, through whom we have now received reconciliation." (Rom 5,10f) The same two elements of the redemption are underlined in expressions like "who has reconciled us to himself through Christ." (2 Cor 5,18) This fact is given an even more complete formulation: "For it has pleased God the Father that . . . through him he should reconcile to himself all things, whether on earth or in the heavens, making peace through the blood of his cross. You yourselves were at one time estranged and enemies in mind through your evil works. But now he has reconciled you in his body of flesh through his death, to present you holy and undefiled and irreproachable before him." (Col 1,20ff; Eph 2,13.16)

In these statements the basic plan of redemption is bared. It can be seen that the purpose and the climax of the divine effort are found in the reconciliation of man to God. Man alienates himself from God by his sin, but God continues to love man and takes the initiative to dissolve the enmity between man and himself. To this end the Father sends his Son, who assumes and makes his own a human nature. The God-man, using this human nature and its acts as instruments, eliminates the enmity and effects the reconciliation.

In executing the plan of his Father Christ offered himself in sacrifice to him, and in this way expressed his love and obedience. The sacrifice of Christ had value before the Father; in view of it and the consequent worthiness produced in Christ and in all men, the Father returns to man the supernatural gifts forfeited by Adam. For this reason, Christ's action is said to be *meritorious*. The sacrifice of Christ was used by the Father as an instrument of *liberation* freeing man from the captivity of sin and the devil and for this reason it is called the ransoming or redemption of man. The sacrifice gave a more than adequate compensation for the injury done by sin and is, therefore, an act of *satisfaction*.

Implied in each of these aspects and specific effects of Christ's work is the fact that they were designed to reunite man with God, that is, achieve a *reconciliation*. This is clearly seen in the offering of sacrifice, an action which culminates in God's possession of the victim and, through the victim, of those who offer the sacrifice. Christ's merit gains glorification for himself and through this regains the supernatural life for all men; enlivened by grace, man enters into a community of life with Christ and into friendship with God through Christ and in him. The payment of a ransom for man by Christ involves the liberation of man from sin and the devil, and also the acquisition of man by God; man thus purchased by the blood of Christ is possessed more completely by God, consecrated to God, and made holy in himself. The satisfaction given by Christ is aimed at the elimination of guilt; it opens the way to man's reception of new life and consequent reunion with God.

In each of these effects of Christ's work, it is important to recognize that the positive dimension is the heart of the matter. In light of this fact, it is possible to assess properly the meaning of the resurrection in the plan of redemption. Complementing what Christ *does* in the offering of sacrifice with its effects of merit, liberation, and satisfaction is the Father's work of glorifying Christ and thus reuniting men to himself through Christ. The estrangement from God is eliminated. Man is rejoined to God in Christ in a union of mutual friendship.

CHRIST, THE UNIVERSAL PRINCIPLE OF SALVATION

It is important to note that Christ's redemptive acts were done for the benefit of all men without exception. The Church has firmly rejected any suggestion of limiting the scope of his purpose and work. Jansen's teaching that the values of the redemption were limited to the predestined was rejected. (D1096) Another condemnation was levelled at those who proposed that Christ offered himself only for believers. (D1294) More positively, the Council of Trent declared that Christ was sent "that the Jews, who were under the Law, might be redeemed, and that the gentiles, who were not pursuing justice, might secure justice, and that all might receive the adoption of sons." (D794) In contradicting the teaching of various groups of predestinarians, many particular councils strongly urged the universality of Christ's saving purpose. A typical statement can be found in the Council of Quiersy (A.D. 853): "Since no man is or has been or will be whose nature will not have been assumed in Christ Jesus our Lord, so there is not, has never been, nor ever will be any man for whom he has not suffered." (D319)

All such statements made by the Church reflect faithfully the teaching of the New Testament. St. Paul's strongest declaration is the flat one that God wills the salvation of all men, "for there is one God and one mediator between God and man, himself man, Christ Jesus, who gave himself a ransom for all." (1 Tim 2,4ff) The line of reasoning is that God wills the salvation of all men of whom he is the God and for whom Christ is the mediator. Since this includes all men who have ever been or ever will be, the conclusion emerges that Christ gave his life for the benefit of every human being. Paul also makes the point that the benefits of Christ's obedience are co-extensive with the bad effects of Adam's disobedience. Since the sin of Adam affected every human being, it must be concluded that Paul saw the benefits of Christ's redemptive acts as universal. (Rom 5,18; 1 Cor 15,22; 2 Cor 5,15) St. John's testimony to the same fact is compelling. He speaks of Christ as a "propitiation for our sins, not for ours only, but also for those of the whole world." (1 Jn 2,2) This statement allows of no exception to the benefits of Christ's redemptive acts. Its values extend to all men, whether they are believers or not.

The fact that Christ died and rose again for all does not mean that all are assured of entrance into heaven. This is usually indicated by the Church in statements which assert the universality of the redemptive act. The Council of Trent states that Christ was a propitiation for the sins of all men, and then adds: "But even though Christ did die for all, still not all receive the benefit of his death, but only those with whom the merit of his passion is shared." (D795)

The situation of man upon the completion of the redeeming acts of Christ can be described by saying that personal salvation was within reach. The bonds of sin and the devil were broken, life had been merited by Christ and was available, glory had been given to God in place of dishonor. For any man to take possession of these benefits, it is necessary that they be applied to him through a vital link established between him and Christ. St. Thomas points out that as the sin of Adam is contracted by carnal generation or through this link with him, the merit of Christ is applied through spiritual generation, or baptism, by which men are incorporated into Christ. (*S.Th.*, 3,19,4 ad 3) Incorporation into Christ realizes the potentialities of Christ's headship, makes man a member of the mystical body of Christ, and opens him to receive new life in Christ.

The same situation at the completion of the redemption can be described from the side of Christ by saying that his death and resurrection (the latter a type of the mystery of glorification which ends in his enthronement), established him as a universal cause or principle of salvation, a life-giving spirit capable of bringing all men into direct and vital contact with the divinity. St. Thomas speaks of him as a remedy for sin prepared and able to produce the desired effects when applied (*S.Th.*, 3,49,1 ad 3 and ad 4) His work completed on earth, and now established as a principle of salvation, Christ continues his work of priestly mediation by applying to men the benefits he won during his life on earth. What was begun on Calvary is finished at Pentecost, when in the power of the Holy Spirit men go forth to proclaim that in Christ crucified and glorious all are saved.

CHAPTER SIX

THE NEW EVE

The discussion of Mary's part in the redemption must begin with the initiative of God. God's decision to rescue man from his sinful condition originated in the divine love. It was completely free and unforced. Nor was he obliged to implement this decision in any one way; his infinite love and power could have effected the redemption in many ways. That he chose to accomplish it by the satisfaction of divine justice through the incarnation of the Son was, again, a free decision. God was not compelled in any respect by the nature of man's situation in sin or by his love for man to decree, plan, and execute the redemption as he did. In all its details, circumstances, and aspects, the redemption was freely chosen by God. In view of this fact, it must be recognized that man's only access to information about the redemption is by faith in God who reveals his plan. Preformed notions or preferences about the plan of redemption can obstruct the objective view of the revealed data that the theologian must have. The efforts of the theologian must be directed to the discovery of God's free decisions by examination of these data.

The above remarks are relevant to the investigation of Mary's place in the redemptive plan since it is obvious that God did not need Mary to bring about the redemption. No one can argue from the nature of the situation to any necessary role played by Mary in the work of redemption. The only basis for asserting that Mary did take part in the redemptive work as an associate of Christ is what has been revealed to us. A study of the data leads to the conclusion that God did include Mary in the work of redemption. God used Mary as an instrument of redemption; she had a part in its accomplishment. Associated with Christ and dependent on him, Mary cooperated as an instrumental cause in producing the total effect. Together with Christ and subordinate to him, she is part of the principle of salvation for all men.

THE INSIGHT OF THE FATHERS

In view of the vigorous Protestant dissent concerning Mary's cooperation in the redemptive acts of Christ, and the debate among Catholics about its nature, the theologian must be concerned explicitly with establishing the *fact* of Mary's cooperation. This task is best begun by examining the striking testimony to this fact in the writings of the Fathers of the East. Beginning with Justin in the middle of the second century, Mary is presented as the new Eve. The Fathers work out a parallel between Mary and Eve which corresponds in outline to that between Christ and Adam. This view of Mary as the new Eve has been called by Newman "the great rudimental teaching of antiquity from its earliest date. . . ." concerning Mary. It is certainly the original insight of the Fathers with respect to Christ's mother.

Justin

Justin's testimony is little more than a statement of the parallel. The design of man's redemption paralleled his fall in that both were brought about through the efforts of a virgin. It is implied that Mary provided obedience which led to the incarnation and the destruction of the sin of disobedience caused by the serpent. Eve, on the other hand, had provided disobedience in succumbing to the temptation of the serpent. Eve's effort resulted in death and Mary's in deliverance from death. (*Dialogue with Trypho,* 100)

Irenaeus

The parallel between Mary and Eve was developed at length and its meaning investigated by Irenaeus. Putting it in the context of his redemption theology, the keystone of which is the "recapitulation" or summing up of all men in Christ, Irenaeus explained the parallel as descriptive of the process by which God untangled the situation of man in sin. He saw man's situation as a complicated knot which could be untied only by reversing the process of the tying. Thus, Adam's disobedience was undone by Christ's obedience.

Since Eve had been influential in bringing about man's sinful condition, Mary was influential in freeing him from this condition. "Just as Eve . . . became by her disobedience the cause of death for herself and the whole human race, so Mary too, . . . became by her obedience the cause of salvation for herself and the whole human race." The explanation of the process of redemption as a reversing of the process of sin follows closely: "And so it was that the knot of Eve's disobedience was loosed by Mary's obedience. For what the virgin Eve bound fast by her refusal to believe, this the Virgin Mary unbound by her belief." (*Against Heresies,* 3,32,1)

These lines of Irenaeus are noteworthy for the flat statement that Mary became a cause of salvation for all men. It is important, too, to notice that Irenaeus did not think of Mary's cooperation in the process of redemption as confined to the fact that she is the mother of God. The critical aspect of her cooperation lies in the free consent she gave to God through the angel Gabriel; this was her obedience to the divine will. Her consent was not terminated simply at the incarnation but at the incarnation which she recognized as redemptive. (Mt 1, 21) Her free act of obedience had a redemptive value.

Continuation of Tradition in the West

The Mary-Eve parallel was not developed significantly by the Fathers after the third century but it was frequently repeated. Tertullian emphasizes the contrast between the faith of Mary in God and the trust Eve placed in Satan: "The fault which the one committed by believing, the other by believing amended." (*The Flesh of Christ,* 17) Ambrose called Mary the mother of salvation in contrast to Eve, the mother of the race. (*Epistle* 63,33) Jerome states the case tersely: "Death through Eve, life through Mary." (*Epistle* 22,21) The repetition of this theme was constant through the patristic age. From the middle of the eighth century through the middle ages to the present time there have always been strong voices giving witness to the validity of the Mary-Eve parallel, consequently to the fact that Mary contributed to the redemption of the human race.

While this insight of the Fathers is striking and their testimony is significant in tracing the history of this doctrine and in offering an apologia for it, the theologian should be careful about claiming too much for it. Some theologians argue that it is legitimate to conclude from Irenaeus that he envisioned Mary cooperating not just in the accomplishing of the redemptive incarnation but in the entire process of redemption up to and including the crucifixion. This means that in Irenaeus' theology Christ the redeemer and Mary the coredemptrix (as some term her) constitute a single total principle of redemption. Other theologians are more modest in their conclusions. They maintain that in the thinking of Irenaeus Mary cooperated immediately in the redemptive incarnation and for this reason can be called the "cause of our salvation." They demur, however, at attributing to Irenaeus the idea that Mary cooperated immediately in all the redemptive acts of Christ.

This opinion which claims less seems to be the better founded. The insights of the patristic period into Mary's mission is not a complete statement of the doctrine of coredemption but the beginning of its development. Many elements of the doctrine which came to be recognized and worked out much later are contained in patristic texts but only in a seminal stage. After a long and complicated development of the doctrine, these elements are apparent now; but to say that they were part of the theology of the second century is to go beyond the limits of sound interpretation. These texts—evidence of a startling breakthrough in the understanding of Mary—establish the pattern of development for the doctrine of coredemption.

SCRIPTURAL FOUNDATIONS

The vision of Mary as the new Eve prompts the theologian to pursue the development of this doctrine in the teaching of the Church. But before this part of the study is undertaken, it is well for him to try to determine the inspiration of the patristic insight. His task here is to determine the points from which the Fathers launched their argumentation. There are no explicit references to any specifically coredemptive activity by Mary to be found in the New Testament. Her maternal association with Christ from his conception to his death is obvious enough. That her association with Christ had redemptive meaning and value, however, is not explicitly stated.

Protoevangelium

Many theologians are of the opinion that the promise of a redeemer after Adam's sin (Gn 3,15) was influential in the formulation of the Mary-Eve parallel. God promised to provide an adversary for the serpent. This adversary, identified as the "seed" of the woman, will engage in an absolute struggle with the personification of evil and will completely defeat him. The woman is also said to be part of the struggle; she is established with her seed as the implacable enemy of the serpent. It can be inferred that, as she is associated in the enmity, she takes part in the struggle and in the victory over the enemy. The phrasing of the promise has given rise to many exegetical and doctrinal debates over the course of the centuries.

Much of the difficulty that has attended the interpretation of this verse can be dissipated if it is studied in light of Catholic tradition. The Church in reflecting on these words has seen in them a promise of a redeemer. When the redeemer has been identified as Christ, his redemptive work is described, in the terms of Genesis 3,15, as a struggle against Satan climaxed by his victory over him in the crucifixion and resurrection. The woman of the text presents no problem if her identity is sought only within the boundaries of the text itself; she is Eve. The Church, however, has taught authoritatively that Mary, the mother of Christ, is indicated *in some way* in this verse. Without embarking on a discussion of all the issues involved, it can be pointed out that the Church has recognized Mary in Genesis 3,15. (Bull *Ineffabilis Deus,* 8 Dec., 1854; Apostolic Constitution *Munifentissimus Deus, AAS,* 42 (1950), 768f; Encyclical *Fulgens Corona, AAS,* 45 [1953], 579) This is not to say that Mary's identity as the antitype of the woman of the text is discoverable apart from later revelations and the reflection of the Church on the complete divine message.

Given the fact of some identification of Mary with the woman of Genesis 3,15 and the conclusion that she is associated with Christ in the triumph over Satan, the contrast between Mary and Eve begins to emerge. When Christ is described as the New Adam and his redemptive activity is viewed in contrast to the sinful act of Adam, it can be seen that Mary's cooperation with Christ and Eve's with Adam are at the same time similar and in opposition. (1 Cor 15,45; Rom 5,9.21) "As the human race was sentenced to death by means of a virgin, by means of a virgin is it delivered." (Irenaeus, *Against Heresies,* 5,19,1)

Annunciation Narrative

The Mary-Eve parallel also stresses the obedience of Mary as a corrective for the disobedience of Eve. Irenaeus works out this aspect of the parallel: "As Eve was seduced by the utterance of an angel to flee God after disobeying his word, so Mary by the utterance of an angel had the glad tidings brought to her, that she should bear God in obedience to his word." (*Against Heresies,* 5,19,1) From this passage it is evident that Irenaeus attaches redemptive significance to Mary's response to the angel at the annunciation. Mary's response to Gabriel's message is her submission to the divine will: "Behold the handmaid of the Lord; be it done unto me according to thy word." (Lk 1,38)

Again, in the focus of Catholic tradition, it is possible to see in these words the agreement of Mary to the plan of redemption and the beginning of her association with Christ in its work. Mary's consent went beyond the fact of the divine motherhood and the taking of a human nature by the Son of God; the implications of the angel's description of her son (Lk 1,31ff) were not lost on her; with at least an adequate knowledge of her son's saving mission, she gave a consent which included this mission. Briefly, Mary consented to become the mother of the redeemer, a divine person.

The freedom of Mary's consent is also significant. The angel's message does not merely inform her of what God is going to do; the execution of the divine plan awaits her unforced consent and willingness to cooperate. Mary's free consent was more than an openness to Christ's mission and God's plan for her part in it; her *fiat* was an act of positive cooperation in this first stage of the execution of the divine plan, and thus contributed to the redemption. Thus is Mary's "obedience" an important factor in the accomplishment of the redemption.

Purification

Some inkling of a broader scope of Mary's redemptive acts can be gained from Luke's description of the presentation of Christ and the purification of Mary in the temple. (Lk 2,22–40) The main concern of these verses is to set in relief the testimony of Anna and Simeon to Christ's messiaship. Expressions such as "a sign that shall be contradicted" (v. 34) and "that the thoughts of many hearts may be revealed" (v. 35) indicate the messianic orientation of the entire passage. Christ is acknowledged here as the promised one of God, come to inaugurate the golden era for Israel. (vv. 29–32) In this context, Simeon's words to Mary are particularly significant: "And thy own soul a sword shall pierce." (v. 35)

These words have been variously interpreted. Some have thought of them as evidence of moral fault in Mary, that is a willful doubt of Christ's divinity. Others have seen them as prophetic of Mary's purely maternal grief to come at the death of Christ. But the messianic character of the whole incident exposes the basic dimension of this prophecy of Mary's anguish. It would hardly be necessary for Simeon to point to a grief that would be completely personal to Mary; a mother's sorrow at seeing her son in pain is inevitable and hardly calls for such an explicit observation by the prophet. The meaning of the prophecy is that Mary will be anguished by her son's suffering—which is his vocation—

precisely because she participates in these sufferings. Her sharing in his sufferings will involve a share in their purpose and effectiveness. The passage from St. Luke indicates that Mary's cooperation in the redemption is not confined to her conception and bearing of the redeemer; it extends to his passion and death and involves Mary's association with Christ in these critically redemptive acts. The inference is that Mary's association with Christ in these acts has something to do with their effect in men.

Calvary

The indication that Mary's cooperation with Christ extends to his passion and death directs attention to her part in the crucifixion. St. John notes her presence on Calvary along with two other women and a disciple. (Jn 19,25) "When Jesus, therefore, saw his mother and the disciple standing by whom he loved, he said to his mother, Woman, behold thy son. Then he said to the disciple, Behold thy mother." (Jn 19,26f) Taken in their immediate context, these words seem to hold no more than the solution of the personal problem of Mary's care. Taken in the broader context of the whole revealed message, and seeing it in relation to the protoevangelium (Gn 3,15f) and Luke's accounts of the annunciation and the purification, it is possible to see a deeper meaning in these words. Mary's presence on Calvary would be the climax of her coredemptive association with Christ. It would involve on her part cooperation with Christ in his very act of dying and offering himself in sacrifice to the Father. Mary's acts on Calvary have a universal significance and effect; they develop out of her relationship to Christ and also out of a maternal relationship formed by God between her and all men. This text is significant not for any interpretation put on it by the Fathers in working out the Mary-Eve parallel but for the part it has played in later developments of the doctrine and the prominence it has received in the teaching of the popes.

THE DEVELOPED TEACHING OF THE CHURCH

The Church has not solemnly defined the doctrine of Mary's coredemption. This is not to say that the Church has not taught it. In their "ordinary" or day to day teaching, the popes of the last century have presented this doctrine with increasing clarity and firmness. They have not thereby introduced a novelty but have maintained contact with the stream of authentic tradition. Their contribution has been to work out, under the guidance of the Holy Spirit, the implications of the Mary-Eve parallel, of the designation of Mary as the mother of all men and mediatrix of all graces, and to present these conclusions with uncommon incisiveness. No one of the documents to be discussed represents an exercise of the charism of papal infallibility. All of them are authoritative and call for religious assent, if not divine faith, from Catholics. It may be argued that the cumulative value of this teaching over the course of a century is to mark it off as indicative of the faith of the local church of Rome; but since the faith of the Roman church is normative for the universal Church, there is some basis for attaching a more decisive authority to this teaching.[1]

Leo XIII

The emphasis placed by modern popes on Mary's coredemptive role can be dated from Leo XIII. In his rosary encyclicals, he underlined the reasons for confidence in Mary; and in this connection stated explicitly the contributions made by Mary to the redemption and salvation of all men. "She who was so intimately associated with the mystery of human salvation is just as closely associated with the distribution of graces." (Encyclical *Adjutricem Populi,* 5 Sept., 1895) The nature of this association is spelled out more explicitly by showing the links between her consent to the angel, her presentation of Christ in the Temple, and her presence on Calvary:

> She knew beforehand all these agonies; she knew and saw them. When she professed herself the handmaid of the Lord for the mother's office, and when, at the foot of the altar, she offered up her whole self with her child Jesus, . . . she took her part in the painful expiation offered by her Son for the sins of the world. . . . As we contemplate him in the last and most piteous of these mysteries, we see that there stood by the cross of Jesus his mother, who . . . generously offered

[1] A convincing argument for this point is presented by P. Nau, OSB in "Le magistère pontifical, lieu theólogique," *Revue Thomiste* 56 (1956), 389-412. The authority of Pius IX in the Bull *Ineffabilis Deus,* 8 Dec., 1854 and Pius XII in the Encyclical *Humani Generis, AAS,* 42 (1950), 568 can also be cited.

> her own Son to Divine Justice and in her own heart died with him, stabbed by the sword of sorrow. (Encyclical *Jucunda Semper,* 8 Sept., 1894)

These words are significant for the distinction they make between Mary's coredemptive acts and her cooperation with Christ in distributing the benefits of redemption.

St. Pius X

The same distinction is maintained by Pope St. Pius X when he outlines the chief redemptive acts of Mary. He sees her task in connection with the sacrifice of Christ. By conceiving and bearing Christ she prepared the victim of the sacrifice; her care of him is described as the tending and nourishing of the victim; finally, he speaks of her task "of offering it on the altar at the appointed time." (Encyclical *Ad Diem Illum, ASS* 36 [1903–04], 453) Mary's presence on Calvary is attributed to a constant community of life and labor between mother and son, "and by this community of pain and will between Christ and Mary she merited to become in a most worthy manner the reparatrix of the lost world." (*Loc. cit.*) Then the pope locates Mary in subordination to Christ and gives assurance that her role as mediatrix subtracts nothing from Christ's position as mediator. To put Mary's work of mediation in relief, he shows her unique function in the redemption: "Since she was chosen by Christ to be his associate in the work of human salvation, she has merited for us congruously, as they say, what Christ has merited for us condignly." (*Loc. cit.*)

Benedict XV

The presentation of the doctrine of coredemption gained in clarity and force with the Apostolic Letter *Inter Sodalicia* of Pope Benedict XV. His most trenchant statement concerns Mary's presence on Calvary and the nature of her activity there.

> Thus, she [Mary] suffered and all but died along with her son suffering and dying; thus for the salvation of men she abdicated the rights of a mother toward her son, and insofar as it was hers to do, she immolated the Son to placate God's justice, so that she herself may justly be said to have redeemed together with Christ the human race. (*ASS* 10 [1918], 182)

This statement is by far the most unequivocal presentation of the doctrine of Mary's coredemption, and it is the starting point for the teaching of later popes.

Pius XI

In the Encyclical *Miserentissimus Redemptor,* Pope Pius XI briefly outlined Mary's coredemptive acts: "By giving us Christ the redeemer, and by rearing him, and by offering him at the foot of the cross as victim for our sins . . . Mary became and is known as reparatrix." (*AAS* 20 [1928], 178) His unique contribution to the development of the doctrine lies in his explicit application of the title "coredemptrix" to Mary. This he did in the prayer with which he closed the Jubilee Year: "O Mother of love and mercy who, when thy sweetest Son was consummating the redemption of the human race on the altar of the cross, didst stand next to him, suffering with him as a coredemptrix. . . ." (28 Apr., 1935) It should be noted that Mary is called coredemptrix precisely in connection with her presence on Calvary and because of her activity at that time.

Pius XII

This authoritative interpretation of Mary's presence on Calvary was seconded by Pope Pius XII in what has come to be known as the Marian Epilogue of the Encyclical *Mystici Corporis Christi.* Some emphasis is given to the redemptive implications of Mary's consent to the angel's message: ". . . in the name of the whole human race, Mary gave her consent for a spiritual marriage between the Son of God and human nature . . . she brought him forth as the source of all supernatural life." (*AAS* 35 [1943], 247) Then, after mentioning her part in the miracle at Cana, he brings his thought to a climax:

> It was she, the second Eve who, free from all sin . . . and always most intimately united with her Son, offered him on Golgotha to the eternal Father for all the children of Adam, sin-stained by his unhappy fall, and her mother's rights and mother's love were included in the holocaust. (*Loc. cit.*)

The connection between the Mary-Eve parallel worked out by the Fathers and these subsequent developments is indicated in the Apostolic Constitution *Munificentissimus Deus:*

> We must remember especially that since the second century the Virgin Mary has been designated by the holy Fathers as the New Eve, who, although subject to the New Adam, is most intimately associated with him in that struggle against the infernal foe which, as foretold in the Protoevangelium, finally resulted in that most complete victory over sin and death. (*AAS* 42 [1950], 768f)

Conclusions

From the foregoing survey and sampling of the evidence of Mary's part in the redemption, we may conclude that she did contribute to the redemption and can be called, at least in some sense, a cause of the redemption. This general statement of the doctrine is agreed to by all theologians. All agree to her association with Christ throughout the process by which man was redeemed, at least in the sense that she united her sentiments and sufferings to those of Christ carrying out his saving mission. Beyond this point there is no unanimity among Catholic theologians, and the more detailed and refined explanations of Mary's role are being currently debated.

Some limit very sharply Mary's role in the redemptive process. They would make her contribution to the redemption comparatively remote by saying that it consisted only in her conception and bearing of the redeemer. This is a way of saying that Mary is the cause of the cause of redemption. Her contribution was to provide Christ who is the only direct and immediate cause of man's rescue from sin; she is therefore an indirect and mediate cause of redemption. Her subsequent association with Christ, according to these theologians, had no value for the redemption itself. Men were redeemed in view of the satisfaction and merits of Christ alone; Mary's merits were effective only in establishing her as a dispenser of the graces gained by Christ.[2]

Another opinion, advanced during the last decade, would exclude Mary from any immediate and active cooperation in the work of re-

[2] A fuller explanation of this opinion can be found in George D. Smith, *Mary's Part in Our Redemption* (New York: Kenedy, 1954), pp. 92-99.

demption. Christ alone effected the reconciliation between God and man in the sense that God's friendship was available to man. Mary's cooperation is found in her "accepting" the benefits of his sacrifice and making them available to the members of the Church whom she represented on Calvary.[3]

The most common opinion among Catholic theologians is that Mary cooperated with Christ proximately, directly, and immediately in the achievement of the redemption.[4] Beginning with the conception of Christ and ending with his death, Mary's acts were united with his in such a way that they are genuine causes of the redemption. Christ's acts were infinite in their value and more than sufficient to bring the redemption to completion. Mary's acts had a limited value, were performed with reference to and in dependence on those of Christ, and can be considered effective of the redemption only when seen as forming with the acts of Christ a single principle of redemption. Mary's cooperation did not add anything to the substance of the redemption, but contributed an accidental perfection by way of harmony and beauty to the work of Christ. Mary is not a redemptrix rivalling Christ; she is an instrument used by God in subordination to Christ and as an instrument she contributed something proper, if accidental, to the total effect.

MARY'S COMPASSION

If Mary cooperated immediately and directly with Christ in effecting the redemption, it remains for the theologian to investigate carefully the precise manner in which she cooperated. It has been shown that the redemptive work of Christ consisted basically in the offering of a sacrifice to his Father; this sacrifice had meritorious, liberative, satisfactory, and reconciliatory value for all men. These are aspects of the redemptive activity of Christ and its effects, and they provide an outline within which to study Mary's contribution to the total effect.

---

[3] This opinion is a debatable application of the generally accepted fact that Mary is a type of the Church. It is discussed at length by Cyril Vollert, SJ in *Mariology,* ed. J. B. Carol, II (Bruce: Milwaukee, 1957), 550-95.

[4] Cf. Juniper B. Carol, "Our Lady's Coredemption" in *Mariology,* ed. J. B. Carol, II, 380-81.

Sacrifice

The language of the popes is unmistakable in attributing to Mary some part in Christ's sacrifice. They refer to her immolation of her Son (Benedict XV) and to her offering him at the foot of the cross as a victim (Pius XI); in this way she is said to have redeemed the human race with Christ. Two conclusions emerge from these descriptions of Mary on Calvary. The first is that her suffering and grief there were not merely personal to her; she was on Calvary in an official capacity and her agony had universal repercussions, bringing some benefit to every human being. The second conclusion is that Mary's activity on Calvary was in some way sacrificial. The more precise explanation of this sacrificial activity is debated.

Some theologians argue that the proper agent of a sacrifice is a priest, that Mary was invested with the priesthood by becoming the mother of God, and that she offered Christ the victim while exercising this priestly office. This view is contradicted flatly by another group which denies that Mary is a priest in any proper sense and that her acts on Calvary were strictly sacrificial. The latter position is more in keeping with the Church's reluctance to refer to Mary as a priest and is generally regarded as the sounder of the two opinions.

While Christ was the only officiating priest on Calvary, Mary's part in the offering of this sacrifice is considerable. St. Pius X pointed out Mary's motherly offices in terms of sacrifice, saying that she prepared and tended the victim. (Cf. p. 97.) This constituted a remote cooperation in the sacrificial action. A more proximate cooperation is also linked with her motherhood. Mary could not carry out the precise work of a priest; but she was capable of offering him to God in a unique way because she was his mother. This offering by Mary did not involve any external rite or visible sign; it is not sacrificial in the strict sense if these elements are thought essential. But Mary's interior dispositions, characterized as Christ's were by universal love and perfect obedience to the Father, were perfectly oriented to sacrifice and enabled her to share in her own way in Christ's offering of himself. Mary's way of sharing in this sacrifice was singular because of her motherhood. As Christ's mother, she had maternal rights over him and was able to express her dispositions by abdicating or giving up these rights. (Benedict XV; cf. p. 97.) This was a very specific and unique gift to God. The giving of it undoubtedly placed Mary in a position of active participation in the sacrifice of Christ.

Merit

That Mary's activity contributed to the redemption by way of merit is made clear enough by St. Pius X. (Cf. above, p. 97.) He distinguishes between condign and congruous merit and asserts that Mary's congruous merit is co-extensive with Christ's condign merit. This general statement has to be qualified by a fact which will be explained in more detail later, viz., Mary did not merit for Christ or for herself; but her good acts, particularly her suffering with Christ, had the effect of earning graces for all other men. This is not merely to say that like the other saints she earned the distribution of graces gained by Christ; her acts had congruous value in what is called the acquisition of the graces, or in the work of redemption itself.

Several aspects of Mary's meritorious activity call for comment. It should be noted that her sanctity was uniquely exalted from the first moment of her existence (her being conceived immaculate, that is). Theologians say of her fullness of grace at that time that it exceeded the holiness of all other humans. Nor was her holiness marred by any moral fault or imperfection. Given this singular sanctity, it is to be expected that her good acts would be especially pleasing to God and worthy of reward. But the richness of her merits does not explain the fact that they were beneficial to all men, that they could have a part in regaining for the human race as a whole the gifts lost by Adam. It is vital in explaining the merit of Christ to show that he was the head of the human race, competent to act for all men and eligible to receive for them (since they are in him) the dispositions that qualify for reward from God. Mary does not have this precise relation to all men, a fact which at first blush seems to render impossible any theory of the universality of her merit.

The answer to this problem lies in the fact that while Mary is not the head of the human race and consequently not the head of the mystical body, it cannot be said that she is just another member of the race or of the body of Christ. She is the mother of Christ the redeemer, and forever associated with him in the work of redemption. This fact marks her off from all other human persons; it gives her unique status and an official position in the human race. This is usually indicated by saying that because she is the mother of God she is also the mother of all men. While she needed redeeming like the rest of men, her divinely fashioned relation to Christ and association with him gave her merits unique scope. As Eve, "the mother of all the living" (Gn 3,20), could affect all men by reason of her special status in the human race, Mary, the mother of all men in virtue of her motherhood of him who has all humanity for his brothers, could likewise affect the entire race. Mary's merits were unique. They were subordinate to Christ's and therefore different; on the other hand, they differed from the merits of other members of the race since they were directed to the acquisition of graces in association with him, not merely with the distribution of graces already acquired.

Mary was united with Christ by the divine disposition to form one principle of merit. The immediate effect of the acts of Mary and Christ was to produce a disposition or worthiness of reward. The critical disposition is in Christ. He is the head of the race; all men being in him are thereby disposed to share in his fullness of grace. Mary's ability to cooperate in the distribution of Christ's graces to all men resulted from their joint meritorious activity. Both of them contribute in their respective ways to produce the effect of redemption; the effect is verified in each of them in the way that is proper to each. Through them, every human being is affected.

Liberation

The freeing of man from the slavery of sin and devil is an important aspect of Christ's redemptive work. It is possible to recognize Mary's contribution in this area. Since Eve had been directly instrumental in the enslaving of man, Mary can be expected to have had a part in his release. Christ's payment of a ransom by his death—the shedding of his blood—is obviously shared in by Mary who suffered with him. Like the other effects of his redemptive work, the liberation of man from slavery is somehow within Mary's competence because she is the mother of God and the associate of Christ.

The rescue of man from the devil by Christ and Mary emerges

from the traditional interpretation of Genesis 3,15. The hostility between Christ and Satan is shared by Mary; and she takes part in the complete triumph of Christ over Satan. However this triumph be explained, the sacrificial death of Christ was decisive in bringing it about. Mary took part in this sacrifice of his in her unique way, that is, by offering Christ in a maternal way to his Father. Joined to the offering of Christ by himself, this act of Mary had the effect of contributing to the liberation of man. Thus Mary's part in the sacrifice of Christ included her contribution to the *lýtron* or ransom paid for the release of man from slavery.

Reconciliation

Since the purpose of Christ's redemptive activity was the reconciliation of man and God, it must be concluded that Mary shared this purpose with Christ and that her coredemptive acts promoted the achievement of the effect. Both Pius IX (Bull *Ineffabilis Deus,* Dec. 8, 1854) and St. Pius X have said that "with her only-begotten Son she is the most powerful mediatrix and conciliatrix in the whole world." (Encyclical *Ad Diem Illum, ASS* 36, [1903–1904] p. 453) In the explanation of the various aspects and effects of Christ's redemptive activity, it has been pointed out that his acts by their nature tended to the reunion of the sinner with God. While Mary's cooperation with Christ's activity is not on the same level and did not have an equal value, it did enter into all these aspects of the complete redemptive work and may be said to have tended to the reunion of fallen man with God.

Satisfaction

If Mary's association with Christ included the gaining of merits, it is to be expected that it also involved the making of satisfaction. Like Christ's merits, his satisfaction was more than adequate to meet the requirements of justice. His acts were far more pleasing to God than the sins of men were hateful, and there is no intrinsic need of their being completed by the acts of Mary. But, as Christ and Mary formed one principle of merit, so they made up one principle of satisfaction.

It must be recognized that in the making of satisfaction, Mary is inferior to Christ and intrinsically dependent on him. Only Christ can make condign satisfaction, divine person that he is at the root of his manhood. Mary's acts satisfy congruously because God wills to accept them as sufficient; of themselves they are limited in value and could not equal the offense given to God by sin. Moreover, to keep Mary's activity in perspective it must be remembered that her very ability to make satisfaction, even congruous satisfaction, depends upon the satisfaction made by Christ. (*S.Th.*, 3,1,2 ad 2)

Like her works of merit, her works of satisfaction have a universal effect because she is the mother of God and the associate of Christ. This position in the human race is basic in the execution of the divine decree which makes Mary's acts a subordinate principle of satisfaction in the work of redemption. She is related to all men as their mother; her acts will have effects in all her children. Mary herself received the benefits of the satisfaction of Christ. Given that fact, her works of satisfaction, related to those of Christ, had unique value and range. All men can look back to Christ and Mary for bringing this critical aspect of the redemption to completion. Like her son, she freely accepted the responsibility of discharging man's debt to God and accepted the agonies of the passion to that end.

Mediatrix of All Graces

The doctrine of cooperation in redemption outlined here belongs to a fuller picture of Mary as the mediatrix of all graces. This description of Mary includes her association with her son in the work of redemption completed in his time on earth, and also her association with him in the heavenly work of salvation, or making the redemption operative in the lives of individual men. This could mean that all the graces available to men and possessed by them come to them through the offices of Christ *and* Mary. The one mediator between God and man and his mother would have been joined in this work from the moment of the incarnation and thus form one principle of mediation.

Subordination of Mary

Several rather obvious problems emerge from this assertion. The first is the apparent equality with Christ attributed to Mary. The difficulty is compounded by the contradiction implied in St. Paul's firm statement, "For there is one God and one mediator between God and man, himself man, Christ Jesus. . . ." (1 Tim 2,5) Any defense or explanation of Mary's mediatorial role must strongly affirm not only the primacy but also the uniqueness of Christ in this regard and deny any equality between Christ and Mary. Christ alone is the perfect mediator between God and man, and this by reason of the hypostatic union of natures. (See above, pp. 25-27.) He alone is perfectly "in the middle" between God and man, uniting both extremes in his person and capable of offering the infinite sacrifice which will actually reunite man with God. These facts are beyond any question. Nothing can be subtracted from them. Any place Mary has as mediatrix must be explained within the boundaries of these facts.

That Mary can be called a mediatrix at least in some sense can be seen in her unusual status in the race. She is human and therefore distinct from God; but she is also the mother of God and adorned with a transcendent holiness. These facts can be said to put her also "in the middle," as between humanity and her divine son. One with men, she is nevertheless superior to them and in that sense removed from them. Distinct from God, she is nevertheless, because of her unique supernatural dignity, closer to God than any human person. Her competence to act for all men before God and to represent God among men can be found in her relationship to Christ the head of the human race. Through him she has a special status in the human race and a relationship to all its members. Thus a basic competence to mediate is found in Mary.

But Mary's position as mediatrix and her mediation are intelligible only when seen in dependence on Christ the mediator. Her position in the human race and her superior holiness are derived from him. She does not have these foundations of mediation by any native right but only because of her unique relationship with Christ. Through him she is related to the other persons in God and to all men; from him she has received the supernatural gifts which make up her holiness. Nor can her work of mediation be understood as independent of Christ's work. Christ's mediation is essential, the substance of the work of redemption; Mary's work is not necessary, adds nothing substantial to Christ's work, and is designed to be evaluated only as an accidental modification of the work of Christ. The efficacy and worth of Mary's mediation can be measured only in its relationship to the mediation of Christ to which it is essentially subordinated.

The doctrine of coredemption cannot mean that Christ and Mary were equal partners in the redemption. Mary's contribution was secondary to Christ's, dependent on it and in no way isolated from it. Mary is not another, autonomous mediator but the divinely constituted associate of Christ in his work of mediation. It may be said that she is the inferior and dependent element in the one work of mediation which is essentially the work of Christ.

Mary's Redemption

Another problem encountered in the explanation of Mary's coredemptive activity is the undeniable fact that she herself needed to be saved. Christ was in no way subject to the universal liability to sin. He possessed the fullness of grace as his right from the beginning of his human existence. Mary was immaculately conceived and full of grace from the first moment of her existence, but in her case this was a privilege freely given by God and in view of the foreseen merits of Christ. Mary was not freed from sin but preserved from it by the redemptive acts of her son. She was therefore redeemed by him. The question arises how she can be at the same time a co-operator in the work of redemption and its chief beneficiary.

It must immediately be pointed out that Mary could not have cooperated in her own redemption; that which she received from the redemption was the very basis for her cooperation. It must be granted, too, that the work of Christ is indivisible in itself and in its immediate effect, which is the propitiation of God. But it is possible to distinguish various terminations of the work of Christ. Insofar as it terminated in the singular, preservative redemption of Mary, the work of redemption was that of Christ alone. Mary's efforts had no effect in the work of redemption as it was terminated in herself. But insofar as the redemption was beneficial to all others, Mary's efforts were effective; it can be said that Mary cooperated in the work of Christ as it had its effect outside herself.

Instrument of Divinity

Mary's coredemptive activity must be seen in the context of the divine initiative. She did not intrude on the redemption. She and her efforts were an integral part of God's plan, used by him as instruments to give an accidental beauty and symmetry to the work of redemption.

Unlike Christ's human nature, Mary is not a *conjoined* instrument of the divinity. She is not substantially united to God. This immediately implies her subordination to Christ as an instrument. It indicates that there are necessary differences between God's use of *her* and the human nature of Christ. As an instrument Mary is, like Christ, free under the influence of God. God's employment of her is never violent; it is always within the boundaries of rational nature. Some emphasis is given to this fact in the annunciation narrative, where it is made clear that Mary made her own the purposes and plans of God. Again, like Christ, Mary is under continuous divine influence, sharing in the power of the infinite principal agent and cooperating in the production of effects that are far beyond her native powers. God's use of Mary, therefore, should not be regarded as intermittent; all the actions and sufferings of her life, at least from the moment of the incarnation to the death of Christ, were used by God to bring about the total effect. Quite obviously, she is a *separated* instrument. Her acts, therefore, have an unusual but limited value. Her instrumental action, not being on the same level as Christ's, made an essentially different contribution to the total effect.

God's use of Mary entered into all the aspects of redemption. As every effect bears the impress of the instrument used to produce it, the redemption bears the impress of Mary as well as that of Christ. Mary's impression on the total effect, however, is confined to a meritorious causality. The documents of the Church from which her part in the redemption can be known provide no evidence for viewing her work in any other way. Her cooperation in the distribution of the graces merited in the redemption is another matter. Theologians are currently debating whether her part in this process is confined to intercession or is more direct.

The Spiritual Mother of All Men

The doctrine of coredemption provides some insight into the traditional title, "Mother of Men," given to Mary by the Church. Our Lady's coredemptive activity is basically aimed at the reunion of God and man, which includes the return to man of the supernatural gifts lost by Adam. The reunion of God and man means that man is brought to life again, is made capable of possessing God in a supernatural way and of knowing and loving him supernaturally. A woman who thus cooperates in the production of life is the mother of the one brought to birth. Mary's motherly offices come to a still fuller stage in her actual distribution of all graces to men, whereby she cooperates in a subordinate and womanly manner in the actual supernatural birth and nourishment of each one. But her position as the universal and spiritual mother of all men was established by her cooperation with Christ in first gaining and then making available the supernatural life of grace.

Suggested Readings

CHAPTER ONE

Gelin, Albert, *The Key Concepts of the Old Testament,* tr. George Lamb (New York: Sheed and Ward, 1955), pp. 36-63.

Grossouw, William, *In Christ,* tr. Martin W. Schoenberg (Westminster, Md.: Newman, 1952), pp. 15-33.

Lyonnet, Stanislas, "Conception paulinienne de la Rédemption," *Lumière et Vie,* 7 (Mars, 1958), 35-66.

————, *Theologia biblica Novi Testamenti. De peccato et redemptione: I. De notione peccati* (Romae, 1957).

Prat, Fernand, *The Theology of St. Paul,* tr. John L. Stoddard (Westminster, Md.: Newman first pub. 1928), II, 47-108.

Richard, L., *Le Mystère de la Rédemption* (Tournai: Desclée, 1959), pp. 203-20; 53-61.

Rondet, Henri, *The Theology of Sin,* tr. Royce W. Hughes (Notre Dame, Ind.: Fides Publishers Association, 1960), pp. 12-38.

CHAPTER TWO

Adam, Karl, *The Christ of Faith,* tr. Joyce Crick (New York: Pantheon, 1957), pp. 296-302; (New York: Mentor Omega, 1962), pp. 335-42.

————, *Christ Our Brother,* tr. Justin McCann (New York: Macmillan, 1946), pp. 38-76; (New York: Collier Books, 1962), pp. 52-72.

Héris, C. V., *The Mystery of Christ,* tr. Denis Fahey (Westminster, Md.: Newman, 1950), pp. 33-52; 90-108.

Lécuyer, J., "La Causalité efficiente des mystères du Christ selon Saint Thomas," *Doctor Communis* 6 (1953), 91-120.

Mersch, Emile, *The Theology of the Mystical Body,* tr. Cyril Vollert (B. Herder, 1951), pp. 197-246.

Prat, Fernand, *The Theology of St. Paul,* tr. John L. Stoddard (Westminster, Md.: Newman), II, 161-179.

Scheeben, Matthias J., *The Mysteries of Christianity,* tr. Cyril Vollert (B. Herder, 1946), pp. 364-400.

Van Roo, William A., "The Resurrection of Christ: Instrumental Cause of Grace," in *Christus Victor Mortis* (Romae, 1958), pp. 71-84.

CHAPTER THREE

Durrwell, F. X., *The Resurrection,* tr. Rosemary Sheed (New York: Sheed and Ward, 1960), pp. 1-58.

Lyonnet, Stanislas, "Conception paulinienne de la Rédemption," *Lumière et Vie,* 7 (Mars, 1958), 35-66.

Vawter, Bruce, "Resurrection and Redemption," *The Catholic Biblical Quarterly,* 15 (Jan., 1953), 11-23.

Richard, L., *Le Mystère de la Rédemption* (Tournai: Desclée, 1959), pp. 61-66; 71-86; 259-64.

Schillebeeckx, E., "Ascension and Pentecost," *Worship,* 35 (May, 1961), 336-63.

Stanley, David M., *Christ's Resurrection in Pauline Soteriology* (Romae, 1961), pp. 171-4; 250-85.

CHAPTER FOUR

Durrwell, F. X., *The Resurrection,* tr. Rosemary Sheed (New York: Sheed and Ward, 1960), pp. 59-77.

Grossouw, William, *In Christ,* tr. Martin W. Schoenberg (Westminster, Md.: Newman, 1952), pp. 35-58.

Lyonnet, Stanislas, "De munere sacrificali sanguinis," *Verbum Domini,* 39 (1961), 17-38.

Prat, Fernand, *The Theology of St. Paul,* tr. John L. Stoddard (Westminster, Md.: Newman), II, 180-213.

CHAPTER FIVE

Adam, Karl, *The Christ of Faith,* tr. Joyce Crick (Pantheon, 1957), pp. 325-36; (New York: Mentor Omega, 1962), pp. 367-80.

Lyonnet, Stanislas, "Conception paulinienne de la Rédemption," *Lumière et Vie,* 7 (Mars 1957), 35-66.

———, "De notione salutis in NT," *Verbum Domini* 36 (1958), 3-15.

———, "De notione redemptionis," *Verbum Domini* 36 (1958), 129-46.

———, "De notione emptionis seu acquisitionis," *Verbum Domini* 36 (1958), 257-69.

———, "De notione expiationis," *Verbum Domini* 37 (1959), 336-52; 38 (1960), 65-75.

Richard, L., *Le Mystère de la Rédemption* (Tournai: Desclée, 1959), pp. 265-70.

CHAPTER SIX

Burghardt, Walter J., "Mary in Western Patristic Thought," in *Mariology,* I, ed. Juniper B. Carol (Milwaukee: Bruce, 1954), 110-17.

Carol, Juniper B., "Our Lady's Coredemption," in *Mariology,* II, ed. Juniper B. Carol (Milwaukee: Bruce, 1957), 377-425

Gallagher, Eugene B., "Evaluation of the Arguments in Favor of Mary's Coredemption," *Marian Studies* 2 (1951), 107-28.

Riley, Lawrence J., "Historical Conspectus of the Doctrine of Mary's Coredemption," *Marian Studies* 2 (1951), 27-106.

ABBREVIATIONS

The Books of the Old and New Testaments

Book	Abbr.	Book	Abbr.
Genesis	Gn	Canticle of Canticles	Ct
Exodus	Ex	Wisdom	Wis
Leviticus	Lv	Sirach (Ecclesiasticus)	Sir
Numbers	Nm	Isaia	Is
Deuteronomy	Dt	Jeremia	Jer
Joshua	Jos	Lamentations	Lam
Judges	Jgs	Baruch	Bar
Ruth	Ru	Ezechiel	Ez
1 Samuel (1 Kings)	1 Sm	Daniel	Dn
2 Samuel (2 Kings)	2 Sm	Osea	Os
1 Kings (3 Kings)	1 Kgs	Joel	Jl
2 Kings (4 Kings)	2 Kgs	Amos	Am
1 Chronicles (Paralipomenon)	1 Chr	Abdia	Abd
2 Chronicles (Paralipomenon)	2 Chr	Jona	Jon
Ezra	Ez	Michea	Mi
Nehemia (2 Ezra)	Neh	Nahum	Na
Tobia	Tb	Habacuc	Hb
Judith	Jdt	Sophonia	So
Esther	Est	Aggai	Ag
Job	Jb	Zacharia	Za
Psalms	Ps(s)	Malachia	Mal
Proverbs	Prv	1 Machabees	1 Mc
Coheleth (Ecclesiastes)	Coh	2 Machabees	2 Mc

In the enumeration of the Psalms, the first number follows the Vulgate, the number within brackets, the Hebrew text.

Book	Abbr.	Book	Abbr.
St. Matthew	Mt	1 Timothy	1 Tim
St. Mark	Mk	2 Timothy	2 Tim
St. Luke	Lk	Titus	Ti
St. John	Jn	Philemon	Phlm
Acts of the Apostles	Ac	Hebrews	Heb
Romans	Rom	St. James	Jas
1 Corinthians	1 Cor	1 St. Peter	1 Pt
2 Corinthians	2 Cor	2 St. Peter	2 Pt
Galatians	Gal	1 St. John	1 Jn
Ephesians	Eph	2 St. John	2 Jn
Philippians	Phil	3 St. John	3 Jn
Colossians	Col	St. Jude	Jude
1 Thessalonians	1 Thes	Apocalypse	Ap
2 Thessalonians	2 Thes		

Apocrypha and Qumrân Material

Book	Abbr.	Book	Abbr.
Henoch	Hen	Testament of the Twelve Patriarchs	Test
Jubilees	Jub	Manual of Discipline	MD
Psalms of Solomon	Ps Sol		

Other Source Material

Acta Apostolicae Sedis [Acts of the Apostolic See] — *AAS*

Ancient Christian Writers, ed. J. Quasten and others — *ACW*

Acta Sanctae Sedis [Acts of the Holy See] — *ASS*

Codex Iuris Canonici [Code of Canon Law] — *CIC*

Denzinger-Bannwart-Schönmetzer, *Enchiridion Symbolorum*, 32d ed. [Handbook of the Creeds] — D

Patrologia, series graeca, ed. J. P. Migne — *PG*

Sacrorum Conciliorum nova . . . Collectio — *Mansi*

Patrologia, series latina, ed. J. P. Migne — *PL*

Summa contra Gentes S. Thomae Aquinatis — S.C.G.

Quatuor Libri Sententiarum Petri Lombardi [Four Books of Opinions] — *Sent.*

Summa Theologiae S. Thomae Aquinatis — S.*Th.*

Supplementum tertiae partis Summae Theologiae (Ottawa ed. 1941) — *Suppl.*

The Church Teaches, ed. J. Clarkson and others — *TCT*

INDEX

S

T

U

V

W